Claude Simon's Mythic Muse

Claude Simon's Mythic Muse

by

Karen L. Gould

French Literature Publications Company
Columbia, South Carolina
1979

For my Parents

TABLE OF CONTENTS

ACKNOWLEDGMENTS

For their encouragement and critical insights, I am deeply grateful to Professors John V. Murphy and LaVonne Bussard, whose careful reading and helpful comments proved invaluable. In addition, I wish to thank the Woodrow Wilson Foundation and Bucknell University for their financial support in the preparation of the manuscript. Thanks are also due to Mrs. Kay Beaver for her dependable technical assistance. Most of all, I am indebted to Professor Randi Birn for her inspiration, wise counsel, and continuing friendship.

. . .every culture that has lost myth has lost, by the same token, its natural, healthy creativity. Only a horizon ringed about with myths can unify a culture. The forces of imagination and of Apollonian dream are saved only by myth from indiscriminate rambling. The images of myth must be the daemonic guardians, ubiquitous but unnoticed, presiding over the growth of the child's mind and interpreting to the mature man his life and struggles. Nor does the commonwealth know any more potent unwritten law than that mythic foundation which guarantees its union with religion and its basis in mythic conceptions.

Nietzsche, The Birth of Tragedy

INTRODUCTION

Since the publication of *Le Vent* in 1957, Claude Simon has been increasingly associated with such celebrated proponents of the *nouveau roman* as Alain Robbe-Grillet, Michel Butor, and Nathalie Sarraute. Yet recent critics, both at home and abroad, have become more and more cognizant of the distinctly different literary paths taken by each of the principal founders of France's New Novel. One has only to compare an ambitious work like Robbe-Grillet's *Projet pour une révolution à New York* with Mme Sarraute's equally original novel, *Les Fruits d'or,* or Claude Simon's *Les Corps conducteurs* to appreciate the need for a more demanding critical stance, one that responds to the remarkable variations that exist in this current generation of experimental fiction. The proceedings of the 1971 colloquium at Cerisy-la-Salle on the "Nouveau roman: hier, aujourd'hui" further substantiate the acknowledgment of such widespread diversity, which the authors themselves readily recognized.

Since the advent of the "Midnight" writers,[1] in-depth studies and essay collections have given considerable attention to the individual works of Robbe-Grillet, Butor, and Sarraute. This critical interest has been sparked, at least in part, by each writer's out-spoken commitment to and explanations of the revolutionary nature of the New Novel. Unlike his other three contemporaries, however, Claude Simon has rarely been pre-occupied with the promulgating of broad new aesthetic theories and ideas. This fact alone may account for an evident lacuna in Simon criticism during the sixties, which was limited primarily to plot summary, analyses of particular stylistic techniques, and, all too often, superficial thematic commentary that usually acknowledged Simon's obsession with death and decay, but did little to explain their function within his work. Yet curiously enough, Simon's novels have long been considered the most densely metaphorical and illuminating experiences to emerge from this new tradition of French writers.

But with the recent publication of his fifteenth book, *Leçon de choses*, (1975), Claude Simon is finally beginning to receive the critical recognition he deserves as one of France's leading contemporary novelists. This upsurge of interest is evidenced by still another colloquium at Cerisy-la-Salle in 1974, which devoted its entire proceedings to the discussion of "Claude Simon: Analyse, Théorie." Unfortunately, however, critics over the past five years have continually devoted more and more of their efforts toward inquiries into the formal properties operating in Simon's novels, often at the expense of potentially enlightening commentary on the content. Undoubtedly, this trend is due, in large part, to the current critical fascination with structural components in the *nouveau roman.* There is certainly no question that structural analysis can perform a vital role in clarifying an otherwise opaque Simonian text, especially when this analysis is executed by such perceptive New Novel critics as Ludovic Janvier, Françoise Van Rossum-Guyon, and Jean Ricardou, all of whom have singled out and explored numerous examples of Simon's complex linguistic and structural designs. Yet until quite recently, relatively few critics had discussed his work as a comprehensive poetic expression.

To further this end, a number of critics and scholars, like J. A. E. Loubère,[2] are beginning to examine more carefully the variety of significant imagistic and thematic patterns that contribute to an over-all appreciation of both form and content in Simon's fiction. One of the most pertinent of Simon's image/ theme patterns takes its shape through the intricate interweaving of mythological and archetypal allusions and motifs. This study will consider selected mythic imagery and themes from three specific novels as they relate to a substantially more profound concept of myth in Simon's work since these images and themes emerge from a deep pool of material found in both earlier and subsequent fiction.

La Route des Flandres, Histoire, and *La Bataille de Pharsale,*[3] which are among the most widely acclaimed of Simon's novels and in which a specific nucleus of fictional characters reappear, all follow the convoluting inner movements of a narrative consciousness as it skips back and forth amid perceptions, thoughts, fantasies, and remembrances of key events in the past. If not already familiar with many of the techniques of the *nouveau roman,* readers of Claude Simon may be initially disturbed by each of the three narrator's seemingly chaotic presentation of reality. Inconsistencies increase as Simon's novel progresses because the narrator modifies, changes, and continually questions his own evaluations. Hence we are sometimes unable to distinguish fact from fiction or dream in the mind of his narrators so that we too are led to wonder with the narrator in *La Route des Flandres:* "mais l'ai-je vraiment vu ou cru le voir ou tout simplement imaginé après coup ou encore rêvé" (*RF*, 314)?

The presentation of reality as disorderly and disjointed is an essential part of both form and content in the *nouveau roman*. "La vie," explains Jean-René Huguenin, "ne paraît claire qu'à ceux qui ne l'interrogent pas. Avec le sens de la question, nous avons retrouvé celui du mystère. Certes, nous désirons toujours la lumière, mais moins sûrs de la posséder que de la poursuivre, attentifs à toujours laisser sa part à l'ombre, nous avons le respect de l'inexplicable, nous subissons volontiers le charme incertain des signes, et le forfait nous émerveille."[4] This element of disorder or chaos has been underscored time and again in the thematic treatment of Simon's work. Yet what this study seeks to demonstrate in particular is that, in the face of the apparently pervasive disorder reflected both in consciousness and in human experience, an underlying continuity persists throughout Simon's novels that recognizes the significance of ritual, repetition, and the possibility of transcendence in the activities of our daily lives.

Although the findings of this study relate specifically to *La Route des Flandres* (1960), *Histoire* (1967), and *La Bataille de Pharsale* (1969), they are in many ways equally applicable to Simon's earlier and later fiction. Certainly one can readily argue for the existence of archetypal figures in works as early as *Le Tricheur* (1945) or *Gulliver* (1952), despite the fact that the realistic tenor of description in these early novels inhibits an abundant use of elaborate mythological references. It is not until *Le Vent* (1957) and *L'Herbe* (1958) that the writer begins to significantly alter the descriptive quality of his prose as realistic depiction yields to an expanding metaphorical realm, increasingly rich in interpretive possibilities. Loubère views this gradual change in descriptive emphasis as a way in which "passage[s] of descriptive realism can shift from the 'idea' or signified content to the signifier or sign, with its multiple and intertwined ramifications."[5]

During the years separating *Le Vent* and *Leçon de choses*, Simon's interest in mythological motifs and archetypal symbols becomes more and more central to the meanderings of each narrative consciousness. Ordinarily, such archetypal and mythological imagery emerges from initial encounters with the worlds of love, war, nature, and organized society because they incorporate virtually all of the main characters' essential life experiences. These mythic settings appear to be the only stable elements in an otherwise perpetually changing universe. Moreover, the imagery employed reveals a complex statement on myth in Simon's fiction that consciously recognizes the survival of a dynamic system of ritualistic elements, mythological themes, and archetypal symbols within the modern psyche, thereby uniting men in archaic societies with the inhabitants of our modern metropolis.

A definition of the terminology used is helpful before proceding with an analysis of the properties of myth and mythmaking in Simon's novels. By "mythological," I mean those images and themes that refer to a particular set of myths from a given society, such as Greek, Roman, and Judeo-Christian mythology, or even the contemporary mythology of an established literary giant like Proust. I will use the term "archetypal" to denote those characteristics that we normally associate with the typical and timeless human behavioral patterns, such as the enduring image of the nourishing mother, the betrayed lover, or the wise teacher. In his excellent study of *Mythology in the Modern Novel,* John J. White contends that "no particular myth can present us with the archetype itself, since it denotes the configuration or discernible pattern of attributes common to a number of paradigmatic myths. Far from being historical, the archetype, as used in the accepted technical sense in anthropology, literary criticism and certain schools of analytic psychology, signifies something timeless: a kind of scientific category derived from comparative mythology."[6] This definition seems to be a particularly useful way of distinguishing between the mythological and archetypal imagery encountered in Simon's work.

In order to avoid the plethora of ambiguous definitions established by recent enthusiasts of "myth criticism,"[7] a distinction must be clearly made at this point between the terms "mythological" and "mythic." As I have already indicated, the term "mythological" will refer strictly to those imagistic and thematic elements that can be *overtly* attributed to a specific historical mythology. In contrast, the term "mythic" will denote a symbolic psychological dimension that points toward the universal rather than the particular in human experience. In principle, the interweaving of mythological references and archetypal figures or settings in Simon's novels constitutes a "mythic" mode of cognition that, contrary to what may be termed "rational consciousness,"[8] perceives an underlying oneness in past, present, and future environment. Man, animal, object, and nature itself are broadly associated with types and are easily interchangeable in the eye of the beholder. And, unlike its rational counterpart, the mythic self does not differentiate between subject and object. Having no autonomous identity, the self is experienced and understood only in its identification with the exterior world. Both Time and Space remain fluid, causing past, present, future, here, and there to merge. As a result, there is no ultimate progression in Time, only circular movement and repetition. Mythic awareness thereby transcends the realm of local, personal, and historical activity.

The first three chapters of the study examine consecutively the various components of Simon's mythic awareness as they are found in warfare, male-female relationships, the contemporary city, and the natural environment. Attention is called to the repeated use of mythological and archetypal motifs within these four psychological and spatial settings and to the ways in which these motifs erect parallels between ancient and modern man by constantly referring the reader to familiar analogies. The discussion further distinguishes what manner of universal models emerge from these analogies to archaic as well as more modern symbolisms and interprets their psychological implications for the artistic consciousness behind the work.

The fourth and final chapter raises still broader questions concerning the cognitive function of mythic awareness, particularly as it relates to each narrator's apprehension of the temporal world. The major emphasis of this discussion is placed on the meaning of linear-historical Time, the inherent problems of self-reconstruction to provide a sense of duration, and the significance of a repeatedly recoverable, cyclic Time. Finally, the conclusion takes issue with those who have argued that Simon's work reflects only the disorderly and chaotic forces at work in the cosmos; further, and most important, it affirms the positive value of the mythic vision that allows for the emergence of enduring patterns amid life's universal flux.

NOTES

[1]This nomenclature stems from the fact that all four writers now publish their works almost exclusively at Jerôme Lindon's Editions de Minuit.

[2]Consult J. A. E. Loubère's informative and highly readable study of *The Novels of Claude Simon* (Ithaca, N.Y.: Cornell University Press, 1975). See also John Fletcher's *Claude Simon and Fiction Now* (London: Calder and Boyars, 1975).

[3]These three works will be quoted and identified by the following abbreviations throughout the study: *La Route des Flandres: RF* (Paris: Minuit, 1960); *Histoire: III* (Paris: Minuit, 1967); *La Bataille de Pharsale: BP* (Paris: Minuit, 1969).

[4]Jean-René Huguenin, *Une Autre Jeunesse* (Paris: Seuil, 1965), p. 122.

[5]Loubère makes this comment in reference to Simon's descriptive talent in *L'Herbe*. See *The Novels of Claude Simon*, p. 83.

[6]John J. White, *Mythology in the Modern Novel* (Princeton: Princeton University Press, 1971), p. 44.

[7]A survey of the current preoccupation with myth and literature is an undertaking too vast for the purposes of this particular study. I refer the reader to the following scholars, whose works have been the most helpful in determining the definitional rubric and focus of my investigation: selected works by Joseph Campbell, Mircea Eliade, and Erich Neumann, as well as Georges Gusdorf's *Mythe et métaphysique,* Gilbert Durand's *Les Structures anthropologiques de l'imaginaire,*. Lillian Feder's *Ancient Myth in Modern Poetry*, Hans Meyerhoff's *Time in Literautre*, and John J. White's *Mythology in the Modern Novel.*

[8]The polar opposite of mythic consciousness is "rational," or what has sometimes been termed "empirical-theoretical," consciousness since it

differentiates between all perceived phenomena. The surrounding environment is thereby classified and life in general is compressed into a series of facts and causal relationships through reductive analysis. People, like objects, are particularized, sorted out into various categories. In this way, the self is intellectually perceived and experienced as an autonomous entity, distinctly separate from its surroundings. In addition, the qualities of Time and Space are arithmetically measurable and compartmentalized, causing past, present, future, here, and there to be viewed as isolated experiences. In brief, rational consciousness is interested in a formal elucidation of tangible facts about our world.

I

HEROIC DEFEAT AND DISCOVERY

The search for self in Simon's fiction entails a search for identity amid perceptions, fantasies, and fragmentary memories of past experiences. In many ways reminiscent of Marcel's quest in *A la recherche du temps perdu*, each mental journey narrates a symbolic voyage through the mysteries of life in search of a unifying pattern or center. Venturing into their pasts, his narrators hope to dispel the contemporary malaise which Michel Mansuy has characterized as "le sentiment de l'inexistence du moi aussi bien que du monde."[1] Their point of departure, then, is phenomenological since they recognize that man knows himself only through the verbalization of his encounters in the world. Each narrator's pursuit thereby becomes an archetypal struggle to secure a *self* from detailed accounts of Space, Time, and the World as he has experienced them. Yet like Marcel, he remains at the mercy of a progressively receding past. Hence although his quest may not seem as impressive as those of ancient heroes, it is none the less arduous, for "if anyone—in whatever society—undertakes for himself the perilous journey into the darkness by descending, either intentionally or unintentionally, into the crooked lanes of his own spiritual labyrinth, he soon finds himself in a landscape of symbolical figures."[2]

Leading myth critics generally concur that through mythic awareness "an object or an act becomes real only in so far as it imitates an archetype. Thus, reality is acquired solely through repetition or participation; everything which lacks an exemplary model is 'meaningless,' i.e., it lacks reality."[3] In the Simonian world, archetypes emerge from the narrators' memories and reveries, most often in the form of depersonalized figures or well-known heroes of classical or even more modern mythology. Temporally distant, such phenomena have lost any personal

identity, retaining only the broad outlines of an archetypal con-
figuration or pattern. It is this obscuring of particulars in per-
ceived or remembered phenomena that causes the narrators to
view individuals, places, and things as departicularized, trans-
historical models, invested with symbolic meaning. Moreover,
their extensive use of depersonalization and metaphor empha-
sizes the cyclic as well as the repetitive nature of human and
cosmological history.

Simon's narrators look to their present and past environ-
ments as well as to History in an attempt to determine the es-
sence of their individual being. Yet what they discover is not the
individuality of self, but the archetypal configurations of human
behavior. On the battlefield and in prison, for example, his
narrators witness the coalescence of individual and species.
And as a result, their imagery reflects what is perennially human
since, in times of conflict, the same trials and ultimate fate are
shared by ancient, medieval, and contemporary warriors alike.
Whether in the city, in nature, on the battlefield, or in the arms
of a woman, his narrators enter a realm of archetypal situations
whose essential characteristics transcend the conventional boun-
daries of Time and Space. Consequently, each archetype or
mythological setting functions as an *initiatory guide,* revealing
the hidden, imprisoned, and unconscious aspects of the human
psyche. And initiation, as most mythologists and myth critics
maintain, is intimately related to mythic awareness because it
introduces the neophyte to the perennial truths embedded in
History. Furthermore, the importance of archetypes in Simon's
fiction suggests an overriding philosophical skepticism about
the ability of scientific reasoning to assess accurately the human
condition.

Initiation

"Initiation," as Mircea Eliade explains it, "denotes a body
of rites and oral teachings whose purpose is to produce a decisive
alteration in the religious and social status of the person to be
initiated."[4]   Through initiation, then, the self becomes *other.*
In a contemporary context, we commonly find that ordeals

which engender radical psychological changes form the modern initiatory process since they signify a marked change in man's existential condition, that is to say, in his present understanding and experience of self in the world. For Simon's narrators, the war experience produced a vital psychological change by ending their childhood ignorance of fear, blood, and death. During the chaotic experiences of World War II, they made the discoveries and endured the suffering that constituted their initiation to adult life. As with ancient mythological heroes, "the familiar life horizon has been outgrown; the old concepts, ideals, and emotional patterns no longer fit; the time for the passing of a threshold is at hand."[5] This crossing of a threshold into the unknown world of battle is one of the primary adventures they remember and question in their search for a notion of self.

Like Georges in *La Route des Flandres,* each of Simon's narrators received his early education from a demanding father figure who believed in the absolute ability of words to convey knowledge about the outside world: "tout ce qu'il a à sa disposition c'est seulement cela cette pesante obstinée et superstitieuse crédulité—ou plutôt croyance—en l'absolue prééminence du savoir appris par procuration, de ce qui est écrit, de ces mots que son père à lui qui n'était qu'un paysan n'a jamais pu réussir à déchiffrer" (*RF,* 36). In both *L'Herbe* (1958) and *La Route des Flandres* Pierre, who is Georges' father and the son of an illiterate farmer, appears profoundly mystified by the power of words on a page and assumes that by learning to decipher them he will gradually unlock virtually all of the mysteries of life. However, Georges' adult experiences in war, love, society, and nature have contradicted such rationalistic notions. A printed word or a work of art simply cannot capture the lived experience: "entre le lire dans des livres ou le voir artistiquement représenté dans les musées et le toucher et recevoir les éclaboussures c'est la même différence qui existe entre avoir écrit le mot obus et se retrouver d'un instant à l'autre couché cramponné à la terre elle-même à la place du ciel" (*HI,* 152). Simon himself adheres to Georges' line of thinking when he insists, as he did at Cerisy, that the artist does not reproduce "Reality," but *creates a new reality* filled with its own spatio-temporal settings, individuals, and meanings that did not exist before the work of art itself.[6] The initiate in his fiction is one who experiences an archetypal situation first hand rather than relying on the accounts and presuppositions of others to assess reality.

Simon's narrators entered the battlefield as novices, unaware that a psychological awakening would follow. When they evoke childhood memories, they do so to reflect on their youthful ignorance and to discredit their tutors who naively believed that words would precisely reflect reality.[7] The phrase "je ne savais pas" actually becomes a leit-motif in *La Bataille de Pharsale*: "dard dans la bouche mort dans l'âme je ne savais pas. Sans parler de mots comme passion ou amour même écrits avec un p ou un a minuscules et au pluriel tout juste bons à faire ricaner. Je ne savais pas encore un certain nombre de nécessités" (*BP*, 22). The Latin words the narrators translated in their youth referred to a mysterious, unknown world of violence and death: "l'excitation, l'espèce de fièvre, les mots latins, crus, violents que leur aspect dépaysant, exotique pour ainsi dire, leur sens incertain, chargeaient d'un pouvoir ambigu, multiple" (*HI*, 107). Once in battle, however, they realized that the words themselves were merely shadows of reality: "la mort dans l'âme la peine de mort Je ne savais pas encore pour moi silhouettes grisâtres indistinctes attendant silencieusement dans la pénombre" (*BP*, 18). The allusion here to Sartre's *La Mort dans l'âme* seems to suggest that for Simon, as well as for Sartre, man's confrontation with death plays a paramount role in altering his perceptions of being in the world and precipitates his discovery of the absurd.

In *La Route des Flandres*, Georges also dwells on his lack of preparation and general stupidity upon entering the war. His inexperience and naïveté baffled his companion, Iglésia: "et lui dévisageant alors avec ces mêmes yeux globuleux, ce même regard interdit à la fois doux réprobateur légèrement scandalisé et étonné comme s'il s'efforcait de me comprendre, prenait en pitié mon imbécillité" (*RF*, 47). It is clear that his traditional education based on order and reason left Georges unprepared for the irrational events of the outside world. On the other hand, his friend, Blum, had an obvious educational advantage since his Jewish heritage had given him an almost instinctual understanding of human injustice: "Blum possédait héréditairement une connaissance (l'intelligence avait dit Georges, mais ce n'était pas seulement cela: plus encore: l'expérience intime, atavique, passée au stade du réflexe, de la stupidité et de la méchanceté humaines) des choses qui valait bien trois fois celle qu'un jeune homme de bonne famille avait pu retirer de l'étude des auteurs classiques français, latins et grecs" (*RF*, 169). Blum serves as a new teacher whose lessons constantly underline the discrepancy that exists between words and the world. As Simon had already suggested in *L'Herbe,* man's thirst for knowledge and the elaborate systems invented to communicate that knowledge are, in the final analysis, clever but nevertheless futile attempts to dominate the mysterious, irrational, and unforseeable aspects of life.

Initiation to war means many things in the Simonian world, but above all else, it signifies the revelation of chaos. Yet chaos cannot be conveyed through verbal progression, which is intrinsically linear, nor through the so-called "naturalistic" techniques of modern art. For this reason, the printed word or the scene painted with photographic accuracy invariably fails to capture the tremendous brutality and disorder of the war experience. Reminiscent of Sartre's Roquentin, Simon's narrator remembers his own "sensation de nausée" on the battlefield, where the familiar suddenly became grotesque and incomprehensible: [8]

> Comment? Peur? Si j'avais. . . Je ne sais pas. Peut-être est-ce comme cela que ça s'appelle: une sensation de nausée
>
> ou plutôt comme quand on a un étourdissement ou qu'on a trop bu c'est-à-dire quand le monde visible se sépare en quelque sorte de vous perdant ce visage familier et rassurant qu'il a (parce qu'en réalité on ne le regarde pas), prenant soudain un aspect inconnu vaguement effrayant, les objets cessant de s'identifier avec les symboles verbaux par quoi nous les possédons. . . (*HI*, 177)

Clearly, rationalistic motives cannot satisfactorily account for the fury of human warfare. For the war scenes provide each narrator with his first glimpse of the irrational, a baffling force which sweeps away the secure familiarity of everyday life with "cet aspect insolite brutal irréel incohérent qui est celui de la matière réduite à ses dimensions immédiates se mesurant en termes de force de violence de sang" (*HI*, 209). As Fabrice also discovered in *La Chartreuse de Parme,* the myth of war as it is patriotically sung or poetically narrated bears little, if any, resemblance to the brute physical reality of stricken human bodies. In a very real sense, Simon's initiatory scenarios in wartime become passages to another domain where chance and chaos reign. This shocking world of war is as mysteriously un-familiar to the novice as any underground world or darkened forest depicted in ancient myths.

The initiatory process, however, is incomplete if it is not followed by a psychological *crise de conscience* which, in turn, triggers a radical change in the initiate's concept of self. In mythic terms initiation lays the foundation for a transformation-al process whereby "man becomes *himself* only after having solved a series of desperately difficult and even dangerous situa-tions; that is, after having undergone 'tortures' and 'death,' followed by an awakening to another life, qualitatively different because regenerated."[9] As initiates in war, Simon's protagonists lost their belief in rationalism and human progress once they deciphered the archetypal patterns of the war experience. Order and reason suddenly gave way to the previously tabooed world of the irrational, transforming all of their usual mental deliberations into acts of futility: "mais qu'est-ce que ça pouvait faire la montre l'heure le matin le soir Josué plus tard de nouveau je me demandai alors arrêter de se demander je ne pouvais même plus me rappeler depuis quand ça avait commencé depuis quand nous avancions sur cette route bordée de morts de blessés des siècles peut-être sable sous les paupières," (*BP*, 115-116). The narra-tors must renounce reason if they are to become full-fledged initiates, voluntarily submitting to the irrational in order to accomplish "comme dans un état second des actes d'une façon ou d'une autre contraires à la raison" (*RF*, 193).

The Perennial Battle

La Route des Flandres, Histoire, and *La Bataille de Pharsale* are all set against a backdrop of one or more historic wars. Through association and metaphor, the narrators frequently link their previous experiences in World War II to a series of wars in-cluding the battle of Pharsalus, the French Revolution, the Rus-sian Revolutionary conflicts, World War I, and the Spanish Civil War. Yet because each narrator's mind jumps back and forth in Time, in an almost whimsical fashion, the reader invariably loses track of chronology and historical distinctions. As with other New Novel techniques that negate linear development, this effect is, of course, intentional. Whether the year is actually 1940 on the Flanders Road or 48 B.C. on the plains of Thessaly, what matters is the fact that battles, men, and events are indistinguishable.

To reiterate what has previously been suggested, archetypes point toward a timeless quality, some recurrent pattern in the human condition. In Simon's novels, the battlefield constitutes an archetypal space, a depersonalized location that transcends all temporal and cultural distinctions and, in so doing, creates a continuity between archaic and modern man. Accordingly, Georges hears the cries of an old woman in World War II as the simultaneous lamentations of antiquity and of all those who have known the horrors and the agony of battle: "ses lamentations rythmées, montones, comme une déclamation emphatique, sans fin, comme ces pleureuses de l'antiquité, comme si tout cela. . . ne se passait pas à l'époque des fusils, des bottes de caoutchouc, des rustines et des costumes de confection mais très loin dans le temps, ou de tous les temps, ou en dehors du temps" (*RF*, 63-64). Reminiscing in this fashion over personal exeperiences in battle or gazing at post cards or paintings of war scenes, each narrator depersonalizes the military battles as well as the battlefields. And in so doing, his imagery captures the recurrent and lasting qualities, rather than the peculiarities of any one battle. Likewise, the association of a particular battle with earlier or subsequent wars performs a similar function in Simon's texts. That is to say, battles taking place in various historical periods and cultures appear, not as isolated incidents, but as events existing outside the boundaries of precise, historic time. Whether engaged among brothers, tribes, cities, or nations, human conflict recurs, unchanged, throughout History. Hence, like the ancient myths of the archaic world, this conception of war takes the narrator out of individual-chronological time, evoking an atemporal world freed from the "continuous and irreversible time"[10] of everyday life.

The narrator in *La Route des Flandres* remembers his experiences in World War II while lying in bed with Corinne, the widow of his former regiment captain. Like any single military participant, Georges' vision of war is in one sense, microscopic, since he reconstructs only his own activities in battle, which were mere fragments of the total historical picture of World War II.

Nevertheless, by depersonalizing his own particular battle, Georges encompasses the universality of human wartime experience. For Georges, the war was merely a road, leading nowhere, whose name he never specifies (although Simon does so in the book's title) but which is synonymous in the narrator's mind with death and murder: "cette route qui était quelque chose comme un coupe-gorge, c'est-à-dire pas la guerre mais le meurtre, un endroit où l'on vous assassinait sans qu'on ait le temps de faire ouf" (*RF*, 15-16). Georges rarely evokes the real spatio-temporal location of the road.[11] It remains anonymous, like the unnamed people, animals, and things strewn along it. The student in *Le Palace* (1962) conveys an analogous image of human exile during the Civil War in Spain when he recalls the sea of nameless, interchangeable faces passively awaiting the train departures: "hommes, femmes, vieillards, enfants, l'éternel et millénaire tableau de toutes les catastrophes et de toutes les migrations" (*LP*, 44). The import of these experiences in wartime lie in what took place, rather than when or where it happened. Simon's characters become increasingly aware that a battle's location in Time and Space is ultimately unimportant because the end result is always the same: ditches alongside a war-torn road filled with human corpses, decaying horses, and rusty, abandoned war machines.

As Georges envisions the road, he sees before him horses and soldiers solidified by death as if they had been covered over by a glacier. Finally refound centuries later, he imagines them lying alongside the bodies of old German foot-soldiers and medieval, armor-plated warriors: "semblables à une armée en marche surprise par un cataclysme et que le lent glacier à l'invisible progression restituerait, vomirait dans cent ou deux cent mille ans de clea, pêle-mêle avec tous les vieux lansquenets, reîtres et cuirassiers de jadis, dégringolant, se brisant dans un faible tintement de verre" (*RF*, 31-32). Representative of many war associations in Simon's novels, this passage brings medieval, 19th century, and modern warriors together to lie side by side as participants in the eternal battle. Here, as elsewhere, the narrator stresses the similarities which unite men in their hours of trial.

The equestrian theme emerges as one of the focal points in *La Bataille de Pharsale* and *La Route des Flandres*. In the latter, metaphors aligning medieval combats, modern wars, and horse races frequently appear:

avec les taches bariolées et mélangées des casques, les
queues ondoyantes, la démarche hautaine des bêtes sur
leurs pattes pas plus grosses que de minces brindilles,
apparition, groupe médiéval, chatoyant au loin (et non pas
seulement là-bas, au bout du tournant, mais comme
s'avançant pour ainsi dire du fond des âges, sur les prairies
des batailles éclatantes où, dans l'espace d'un étincelant
après-midi, d'une charge, d'une galopade, se perdaient ou
se gagnaient des royaumes et la main des princesses). . .
(*RF*, 153-154)

Here, the pomp and great expectations of war and horse racing
are the points in common which permit a comparison. The
result is a spatio-temporal disorientation as medieval and modern,
race track and battlefield merge together. "La métaphore,"
explains Ricardou, "est toujours en quelque façon un *exotisme*,
assemblant un *ici* (le comparé) à un *ailleurs* (le comparant).
Utiliser la métaphore comme figure d'expression, revient à
subordonner étroitement l'*ailleurs* à l'*ici*."[12] This kind of meta-
phorical thinking abounds in Simon's fiction, revealing a narra-
tive consciousness that refuses to distinguish between past and
present, here and there, and emphasizing each narrator's obses-
sive concern with the continued presence of human history in
the present moment.

In *La Bataille de Pharsale*, the historical focus shifts back
in time to the ancient battle of Pharsalus in which Caesar de-
feated Pompey on the plains of Thessaly. Yet even though the
central battle is now ancient rather than modern, the descriptive
techniques are similar to those used in *La Route des Flandres*.
The narrator in *La Bataille de Pharsale*, who refers to himself
somewhat obliquely as O., also associates an ancient war with
his own personal experiences in World War II. In his fragmented
narrative, he recounts segments of a trip to Greece, during which
time he attempted to locate the exact site of the ancient battle,
but came away knowing less than when he originally began. Like
other historians before him, he remained dependent on the un-
clear Latin accounts of Lucan (*Pharsalia*) and Caesar (*De bello
civile*) for specific information regarding the battle:

'les indications topographiques, au contraire, sont très
insuffisantes César se borne à dire qu'il a établi son camp
dans les champs (*in agris*) et dans une position favorable

> (ideonem locum nactus); que Pompée de son côté a aligné
> ses troupes en bataille non iniquo loco Il ajoute que
> l'armée de Pompée appuyait son aile droit à une "rivière"
> aux rives escarpées. . . . Comme l'a très bien observé
> Heusey cette description n'est claire que pour qui ne
> cherche pas à l'approfondir' (*BP*, 90-91)

But what was to have been the reconstruction of a particular ancient battle becomes the point of departure for ruminations on personal experiences and on war in general. Recalling the Latin descriptions he has read, the narrator moves immediately forward in time to his own battle experiences, a shift which we can perceive from one paragraph to the next in the following passage:

> 's'élancèrent comme on le leur avait commandé tous
> ensemble et toute la multitude des archers se répandit
> notre cavalerie n'en soutint pas le choc'
>
> Mêmes clameurs sans doute absorbées se diluant
> dérisoires aussi quoique par milliers sous l'étouffant
> ciel blanc et cette mêlée ce tumulte cette confusion
> les hennissements les galops A l'endroit où portait la
> selle les poils trempés de la sueur dessinaient une tache
> marron sombre Dans l'effort que je fis je collai presque
> ma tête contre son flanc. . . (*BP*, 59-60)

There is here, as elsewhere, a kind of common denominator so that, whether in Thessaly or on the Flanders Road, O. can reduce war to its most basic elements: "cette mêlée ce tumulte cette confusion." This three part formula parallels the narrator's earlier comment in *Histoire* that warfare, when confronted in its *immediate dimensions*, is measured in terms of "force," "violence," and "sang" (*HI*, 209). There is a qualitative difference, however, in the two formulas: O.'s perspective is one of a distanced onlooker, removed from the battle and trying to make pictorial sense out of the enmeshed bodies in conflict, whereas the narrator in *Histoire* captures the physical impact of men struggling with or around him. But like most of Simon's protagonists, O. recognizes that in the final analysis, each war, each battle site, resembles a thousand others, for the events that took place in Thessaly have assuredly recurred throughout History on similarly nondescript parcels of land:

tu crois qu'il y a quelque chose à voir?

non   dis-je   Probablement   des   collines   comme
d'autres collines et une rivière comme d'autres rivières
J'ai failli aussi crever dans un endroit où il n'y avait que
des collines et une rivière comme partout ailleurs C'est
toujours comme ça Mais c'est à cause de cette version (*BP*,
31)

What the narrator unwittingly learned from reading Caesar
as a child was not, then, the particulars of a battle, but the
archetypal scenes of human beings engaged in perennial conflict:
"bataille de comment déjà mot qui veut dire les Têtes de Chien
bataille de Pharsale bataille contre les Turcs quel nom avant
après Jésus-Christ pendant comment savoir le sort du monde
pilum frappant entrant sortant dans" (*BP*, 56).[13]   To be sure,
the specifics of any particular battle are insignificant.   What
matters is "le sort du monde," the eternal spectacle of war where
each man confronts his fellow man in the name of Progress,
Reason, and even Justice: "terre gorgée de sang.   AHENO-
BARBUS LENTULUS le sort du monde" (*BP*, 42).

The same metaphorical thinking which correlated horse
racing to war in *La Route des Flandres* also links football to war
in *La Bataille de Pharsale*.   Here again, a battle is associated with
a competitive cultural sport, suggesting that man continues to
act out his aggressive nature in play as well as in warfare. While
searching for the exact location of the fighting at Pharsalus, the
narrator remembers encountering two teams of football players:
"mêlés. . .comme une sorte de bête multicolore de mille-pattes
. . .dans une mêlée confuse" (*BP*, 54-55).   The same words,
"mêlée,"   "confuse,"   "confusion,"   appear   time   and   again
throughout the text to describe players or warriors.   The narra-
tive consciousness wanders freely from memories of football
players to a painted scene of ancient warriors because the two
activities are essentially interchangeable:

plusieurs jambes de joueurs revêtues de bas dispar-
ates rouges jaunes ou vert ployés dans la position de la
course les jambes s'entremêlant se masquant et se démas-
quant tour à tour.   Mêlée confuse aussi de jambes de
chevaux piétant

> un guerrier au corps nu les genoux à demi fléchis
> oscillant d'avant en arrière soit qu'il essaye de parer ou
> d'esquiver les coups qui lui sont portés par un adversaire
> invisible. . . (*BP*, 76-77)

Hence whether the setting is modern Europe or ancient Greece, the narrator views war and competitive sports as similar, aggressive activities. In either case, men win or lose, most often at the hand of chance, like so many of the uncannily close battles in World War II: "le glaive étaincelant qu'il tient dans une main pointé vers la gorge de probablement par un effet du hasard" (*BP*, 61). Without knowing the casual explanations for Caesar's victory at Pharsalus, the narrator knows the essence of that encounter because his cognizance of war is based on personal experiences in World War II, where chance rather than reason played the superior role.

Post cards, political posters, and literary quotations generate a number of similar relfections on war in *Histoire*. As in *La Route des Flandres* and *La Bataille de Pharsale*, the unnamed narrator in *Histoire* moves from one historic period to another, associating his own memories of the Spanish Civil War or World War II with Caesar's military battles, the Russian Revolution, and World War I, which took the life of his father. Thumbing through post cards left in a drawer by his deceased mother, he finds an old photograph of a battlefield that illustrates the history of mankind far better than any history book:

> et encore cette photographie d'un champ de bataille
> prise d'avion. . .et qui illustrait une des dernières pages
> du manuel d'Histoire, comme si celle-ci (l'Histoire)
> s'arrêtait là, comme si la longue suite des chapitres avec
> leurs résumés en caractères gras à apprendre par coeur, la
> longue suite des images qui les illustraient. . .n'avaient
> été écrites, sculptées, peintes, gravées, qu'en vue de cette
> seule fin, ce seul aboutissement, cette apothéose. . . (*HI*,
> 105-106)

The battlefield in the photograph is symbolically anonymous: its depersonalized characteristics typify those of battle sites scattered throughout Time.

Once more, time intervals contract in the Simonian text as

the narrator notes the similarities found in all of the old war photos, regardless of their particular location or date. With relatively minor variations, the twenty black and white post cards of World War I sites depict "la même répétition d'amas, de débris. . .(cette caillasse, cet amas concassé, parfois traversé par une route ou par une rivilère comme si les hommes, les eaux grises, aplanissant ou creusant, s'étaient frayés un passage (mais vers quoi?) à travers cet horizon d'ordures)" (*HI*, 104). In the end, the great expectations of every army disintegrate with the onset of peace and the continuation of widespread injustice. For Simon's narrators, the unanswerable question concerning all military endeavors remains: "frayés un passage (mais vers quoi?)."

The word "apothéose" is a significant one in *Histoire*. It is mentioned twice in relation to a brief quotation from John Reed's *10 Days that Shook the World*: "quel triomphe quel 'apotheosis and millenium without end' massacre quel moutonnement de mourants entremêlés exsangues grisâtres dans le grisâtre crépuscule" (*HI*, 118). The fact that "apotheosis" emerges during the narrator's thoughts on triumph and massacre suggests that Lenin's promises and the narrator's own naive military notions both resulted in unexpected massacre and death. At the same time, his juxtaposition of "triomphe" and "massacre" reveals a deep-seated skepticism concerning the efficacy of war. The historical quotations culminate toward the end of the fourth section of the novel, as the narrator remembers texts that demonstrated how both Communist and Roman leaders drew attention to the sincerity of their quest for peace:

> "Le commissaire du peuple à la guerre grimpa sur l'automobile aidé par de nombreuses mains qui le poussaient en avant et en arrière Trapu court de jambes et tête nue il ne portait aucun insigne sur son uniforme Camarades soldats je n'ai pas besoin de vous dire que je suis un soldat Je n'ai pas besoin de vous dire que je veux la paix"

> commemoravit: il rappela

> testibus se militibus uti posse: qu'il pouvait prendre
> à temoin ses soldats

quanto studio: avec quelle ardeur

pacem petisset: il avait demandé la paix (*HI*, 128)

In addition, the same Latin quote also appears in *La Bataille de Pharsale* when the narrator recalls his attempt to reconstruct Caesar's encounter with Pompey. And likewise, O. sarcastically terminates the quote with "paix," emphasizing the incongruity of such a word when spoken amid preparations for battle and revolution. For him war is an eternal human phenomenon, despite all professed concerns for peace.

It seems, then, that Simon's narrators regard any battle-field as a recurrent initiatory arena in which "everything begins over again at its commencement every instant. The past is but a prefiguration of the future."[14] Although leaders and locations continually change, each battle is a repetition of the same spatial schema and, as such, suspends the passage of Time. History, like myth itself, is thereby reduced to a continual phenomenon of *déjà vu*.[15] This constant emphasis on the recurrence of military conflicts in Simon's fiction would seem to suggest that all battles imitate an archetype and that war itself is an exemplary event.

Archetypal Figures

Men in war, like the battles in which they participate, are similarly depersonalized in Simon's fiction and oftentimes associated with ancient mythological heroes, becoming exemplary models for human behavior in time of conflict. By choosing to relate contemporary deeds with those of ancient civilizations, the narrators further acknowledge traceable universal patterns amid the chaos of History and invite a timeless perspective of the human situation. Like Joyce, Simon uses myth to establish a viable parallel between the contemporary and the ancient, which is an imaginative way of "controlling, of ordering, of giving a shape and a significance to the universal panorama of futility and anarchy which is contemporary history."[16] The difference, as already noted in the Introduction, is that in *Ulysses,* Joyce creates a pattern of references to a specific myth that runs through the novel, whereas Simon interweaves a number of mythological motifs, none of which runs consistently through an entire narrative.

As in ancient struggles, the battlefield in Simon's fiction "is symbolic of the field of life, where every creature lives on the death of another."[17]   The archetypes that emerge from re-membered or imagined war experiences reflect a world besieged by violence and death, the commonn underpinnings of any war-time scenario.   On every battlefield, soldiers wander about con-fused, vulnerable, and ultimately alone, as brotherhood gives way to the irrationality of fratricide.   Each narrator's initiation to war thereby constitutes an initiation to these archetypally significant situations which he must recognize and comprehend if he is to be transformed by them.   And as in dream or in myth, "there is an atmosphere of irresistible fascination about the figure that appears suddenly as guide, marking a new period, a new stage in the biography.   That which has to be faced, and is somehow profoundly familiar to the unconscious—though un-known, surprising, and even frightening to the conscious per-sonality—makes itself known; and what formerly was meaning-ful may become strangely emptied of value."[18]

In battle, soldiers from all ages resemble one another despite their differing socio-political leanings.   Their fate, like their ap-pearance, is impersonal: "leurs voix. . .en quelque sorte im-personnelles, comme leurs uniformes raides" (*RF,* 68-69).   In fact, when engaged in combat, they look more like a mass of indistinguishable   animals   than   like   separate   individuals: "l'ensemble des deux armées dans une confuse mêlée agitée de contractions, de lentes et sinueuses convulsions" (*BP,* 113). Even the leaders, whose busts are later engraved on national coins, resemble one another, with their empty, inexpressive faces: "comme si le même modèle au masque pensif, impitoyable et désabusé posant pour le même peintre avait revêtu chez un costumier de théâtre leurs défroques successives, réincarnations, réapparitions sporadiques d'un unique personnage répété à travers les siècles" (*HI,* 84-85).   Georges often confuses de Reixach, his captain during World War II, with his ancestor who suffered a similar military defeat in the Pyrénées one hundred and fifty years earlier.   Their distinct individuality has faded away with the passage of Time to such an extent that in Georges' mind, both commanders now represent the humiliated leader in defeat who re-emerges to play out his fateful role whenever History deems it necessary: "comme si la guerre la violence le meurtre l'avaient en quelque sorte ressuscité pour le tuer une deuxième fois comme si la balle de pistolet tirée un siècle et demi plus tôt avait mis toutes ces années pour atteindre sa deuxième cible mettre le point final à un nouveau désastre" (*RF*, 79).

Whether Caesar, Mohammed, de Reixach, or Georges' ancestor lead men into battle, the results are identical because the aftermath of all wars is chaos: "le sol parsemé de débris plus ou moins identifiables des casques des boucliers des lances brisées. . .des valises crevées des livres ces détritus que la guerre que toute bataille semble engendrer de façon spontanée" (*BP*, 73-74). If human confrontations constantly recur it is because the same aggressive forces are at work throughout History and because man has always been at their mercy, despite his cultural heritage or technological skills. On the one hand, Simon's narrators seem convinced that there will always be "l'éternel imbécile qui brandira la pancarte et qu'elles [les foules] suivront dans cette sorte d'extase et de fascination où les plonge, comme les enfants, la vue de leurs excréments" (*RF*, 69), and on the other, they acknowledge man's unrelenting desire to transgress the taboo forbidding men to kill each other: "ce même trouble, ce même émoi un peu honteux, tant par la conscience d'un interdit transgressé que par l'aspect presque surnaturel et, pourrait-on-dire, mythologique, de ces combats" (*BP*, 139).

The preface to Part I of *La Route des Flandres* comes from Leonardo da Vinci's paradoxical musing: "je croyais apprendre à vivre, j'apprenais à mourir" (*RF*, 7). On the battlefield, Simon's narrators discovered what millions of warriors before them had also learned, that war is, in fact, an apprenticeship for death: "puisque avant tout la réalité physique de tout combat, de tout meurtre, que ce soit à l'arme blanche, au pistolet ou au canon, c'est celle, immémoriale, rudimentaire et inglorieuse du pugilat des primitifs ou des voyous: des coups assenés" (*HI*, 91). Thus death is viewed as the great equalizer of men since it befalls seemingly stoic captains, like de Reixach, as well as common soldiers, like Wack. The result is anything but glorious for even the most noble: "la chute, le sang, la poussière. . .transformé tout à coup en cette chose indécente et impudique: une ordure simplement" (*HI*, 191-192).

For Simon's narrators, every victim of war becomes a pitiful example of the shocking brutality and irrationality of death. In *La Route des Flandres,* for example, death is as much a surprise for Georges, the onlooker, as it is for Wack, the victim. Georges registers a shock because he is as yet, inexperienced in the ways of battle:

> le visage d'idiot de Wack. . .cette expression ahurie stupéfaite comme par la brusque révélation de la mort c'est-à-dire enfin connue non plus sous la forme abstraite de ce concept avec lequel nous avons pris l'habitude de vivre mais surgie ou plutôt frappant dans sa réalité physique, cette violence cette agression, un coup d'une brutalité inouïe insoupçonnée démesurée injuste imméritée la fureur stupide et stupéfiante des choses qui n'ont pas besoin de raisons pour frapper. . . (*RF,* 88-89)

But as initiates in battle, each narrator must learn to read the *signs* of war on people, places, and things in order to comprehend fully its meaning for them. Like Marcel in *A la recherche du temps perdu,* Simon's reflecting narrators attempt to decipher the signs emitted during their earlier apprenticeship in war, love, nature, and society because "apprendre, c'est d'abord considérer une matière, un objet, un être comme s'ils émettaient des signes à déchiffrer, à interpréter. Il n'y a pas d'apprenti qui ne soit "l'égyptologue" de quelque chose."[19] The signs, however, must be interpreted from first hand experience, not from books or from the opinions of others. For this reason, the translated accounts of ancient Roman conflicts cannot convey the impact of battle to a novice: "ce n'étaient rien que des mots, des images dans des livres, 'je ne savais pas encore, je ne savais pas' " (*BP,* 81). Even the appalling image of the speared Roman soldier, Crastinus, does not communicate the reality of war to the uninitiated: "maintenant il s'élance et presque aussitôt il reçoit dans la bouche un coup de glaive dont la pointe resort par la nuque 'non pas la mort mais le sentiment de ta mort' je ne savais pas encore" (*BP,* 120). Only the immediate experience transmits the terrifying surprise of death, after which point, the literary image takes on a new, and significantly more vital meaning.

Achilles

The figure of the ancient Greek hero, Achilles, arises on several occasions in *La Bataille de Pharsale* to mark the narrator's initiatory death experience in battle. The most obvious reference to the myth of Achilles appears as a prefatory note to Part I of the novel. Here, Simon quotes the twenty-first stanza from Valéry's "Le Cimetière marin," wherein we find several of Zeno's thought-provoking paradoxes concerning the nature of reality.[20] A fifth century philosopher, Zeno of Elea supposedly argued that "what *is,* is a finite, spherical, motionless corporeal *plenum,* and there is nothing beyond it. The appearance of multiplicity and motion, empty space and time, are illusions:"[21]

> Zénon! Cruel Zénon! Zénon d'Elée!
> M'as-tu percé de cette flèche ailée
> Qui vibre, vole, et qui ne vole pas!
> Le son m'enfante et la flèche me tue!
> Ah! le soleil. . . Quelle ombre de tortue
> Pour l'âme, Achille immobile à grands pas![22] (*BP,* 7)

Mobility and immobility function as respective synonyms for life and death or for the conscious and unconscious worlds in each of Simon's novels. O., the narrator in *La Bataille de Pharsale,* aligns his own experience in war to that of Zeno's seemingly motionless Achilles because during his bout with death, he underwent a similar feeling of immobility: " 'je me demandais si j'étais mort je ne souffrais pas je cherchai à remuer mes membres sans y parvenir chacun d'eux pesant des centaines de kilos une tonne ma tête attirée vers le sol par son poids lourde en plomb' " (*BP,* 104). Medicine or love-making can produce a similarly immobilizing effect, as the conscious mind loses its hold on temporal reality. In *Histoire,* the narrator's mind wanders from one memory to another, associating an early drug experience to a later sexual encounter because both events prompted comparable sensations of immobility.

Both Georges and O. evoke multiple images of immobility from their war memories. Their experiences of petrification stemmed from a newly acquired awareness of their own approaching death. Like Achilles, the soldiers on the Flanders Road appeared to be perenially fixed in one place:

tout ce qu'il percevait maintenant c'était le bruit, le martellement monotone et multiple des sabots sur la route se répercutant, se multipliant. . .quelque chose de majestueux, monumental: le cheminement même du temps, c'est-à-dire invisible immatériel sans commencement ni fin ni repère, et au sein duquel il avait la sensation de se tenir, glacé, raide sur son cheval lui aussi invisible dans le noir, parmi les fantômes de cavaliers aux invisibles et hautes silhouettes glissant horizontalement, oscillant ou plutôt se dandinant faiblement au pas cahoté des chevaux, si bien que l'escadron, le régiment tout entier semblait progresser sans avancer. . . (*RF, 30*)

Frightened that they may not escape before the enemy surrounds them, the four horsemen in *La Bataille de Pharsale* have a similar sensation of being frozen in Time and Space: "ils éperonnent les chevaux. Les chevaux prennent le galop, mais il semble qu'ils aillent encore plus lentement qu'au trot, comme s'ils basculaient sur place d'avant en arrière sans avancer" (*BP, 263*).

Thus, Valéry's Achilles becomes a fixed mythological image for Simon's narrators, illustrating the immobilizing effect of approaching death. Totally exhausted, they too felt like stationary mannequins, caught in a temporal limbo between life and death:

je renonçai je ne marchais même plus à la vitesse d'un homme au pas il me fallait même faire un effort pour ouvrir assez mes jambes à l'écartement des traverses je pensai que des milliers des dizaines de milliers de gens étaient passés là assis sur des banquettes lisant leur journal ou un livre regardant distraitement le paysage un type sur une moissonneuse un cheval blanc une charette de foin dans un champ une ferme images figées apparues disparues conservées "Achille immobile à grands pas" (*BP, 84*)

Reminiscent of the motionless presence of the dying Marie in *L'Herbe,* the figure of Achilles is a haunting one for Simon's narrative consciousness, alerting it to the futility of movement in the face of life's immobilizing end: "cette forme futile et illusoire de la vie qu'est le mouvement" (*RF, 245*). Negating the passage of Time as well as movement in Space can only further contribute to a mounting mythic awareness that experiences the underlying oneness of past, present, future, here, and there.

Crastinus

Crastinus is referred to on several occasions in *La Bataille de Pharsale* as one of Caesar's commanders at Pharsalus. He was presumably the first soldier to enter into combat. O. cites both Plutarch and Lucan in reference to the young commander's actions and dreadful death:

> Plutarque et Lucain confirment le fait; cf. Plutarque, Cés., XLIV; Pomp., LXXI: 'Le premier, Crastinus s'élance au pas de course, entraînant derrière lui les cent vingt hommes qu'il commandait'; et Lucain, Phars., VII, 470-473; 'Puissent les dieux te donner non pas la mort, qui est le châtiment réservé à tous, mais, après ton destin fatal, le sentiment de ta mort, Crastinus, toi, dont la main brandit la lance qui engagea le combat et la première teignit la Thessalie de sang romain!'. . .Plutarque (César, LXIV) précise: 'Il reçut dans la bouche un si violent coup de glaive que la pointe en sortit par la nuque.' (*BP*, 235-236)

Like Achilles, Crastinus becomes another fixed mythological image in the narrator's mind. His fate emphasizes man's potential vulnerability while revealing a heightened awareness of death. Looking over the supposed terrain of the ancient battle site, O. watches a team of football players and is once again reminded of Crastinus: "et l'arbitre siffla 'non pas la mort qui est le châtiment réservé à tous mais après ton destin fatal le sentiment de ta mort il reçut dans la bouche un si violent coup de' Du haut de la colline on pouvait maintenant voir toute l'étendu du champde bataille" (*BP*, 67). For O., the figure of Crastinus becomes a truly illustrative archetype because it has meaning for both modern soldiers and ancient heroes. Constantly repeating itself throughout History, the isolated image of the speared Crastinus depicts the eternal irony of human warfare: men forever desirous of immortality, engage in fraternal battle and inevitably meet with death. Regardless of Zeno's clever philosophical arguments about the impossibility of motion, all men eventually come to know pain, immobility, and death. As Valéry's stanza would seem to suggest, the fact that the arrow kills Achilles proves that it moves and that he was indeed alive.[23]

Crastinus is the archetypal leader, much like Georges' ancestor in *La Route des Flandres.* The irony however, with regard to them both, is that they managed to disassociate their cause from the rest of human history, hoping to liberate man once and for all, through their dedication to the side of Justice: "—C'est le dernier combat qui nous reste:—quo confecto—une fois livré,—et ille suam dignitatem et nos nostram libertatem recuperabimus —et lui recouvrera sa dignité, et nous notre liberté" (*BP*, 233). But Simon's narrators have learned from their exposure to Civil War and World War, that no war can definitively liberate mankind from suffering and injustice. Thus, Georges berates his ancestor for his illusions about History and warns that "les révolutions se renforcent et s'affermissent dans les désastres pour se corrompre à la fin, se pervertir et s'écrouler dans une apothéose de triomphes militaires. . ." (*RF*, 222). The rumblings of political turmoil and upheaval do not signal definitive progress or change, merely the continual rise and fall of similar power structures.

The Mythological Cyclops

The dying horse in *La Route des Flandres* is yet another archetype of war in Simon's fiction. Like Crastinus, it too is conscious of impending death and also conscious of those who are responsible for it. But unlike the ignorant soldiers who have not yet been initiated to the horrors of life and the tranquility of death, the horse has a more precise, more comprehensive vision:

> la tête du cheval couché sur le côté semble s'allonger,
> prend un air apocalyptique, effrayant, les flancs annelés
> se soulevant et s'abaissant rapidement, emplissant le
> silence de ce souffle, l'oeil velouté, immense, reflétant

> toujours le cercle des soldats mais comme s'il les ignorait maintenant, comme s'il regardait à travers eux quelque chose qu'ils ne peuvent pas voir, eux dont les silhouettes réduites se dessinent en surimpression sur le globe humide comme à la surface de ces boules mordorées qui semblent accaparer, aspirer dans une perspective déformante, vertigineuse, engloutir en elles la totalité du monde visible, comme si le cheval avait déjà cessé d'être là, comme s'il avait abandonné, renoncé au spectacle de ce monde pour retourner son regard, le concentrer sur une vision intérieure plus reposante que l'incessante agitation de la vie, une réalité plus réelle que le réel. . .(*RF,* 130-131)

This exemplary beast represents all animals who become the innocent victims of human warfare. As the horse approaches death, its eye is the only surviving link with the soldiers who have gathered around. Like an ancient mythological cyclops whose eye absorbs and projects the whole of the visible world, it looks accusingly at its masters: "l'oeil qui semblait vivre encore, énorme, triste, et dedans, sur la surface luisante et bombée, ils pouvaient se voir, leurs silhouettes déformées comme des parenthèses se détachant sur le fond clair de la porte comme une sorte de brouillard légèrement bleuté, comme un voile, une taie qui déjà semblait se former, embuer le doux regard de cyclope, accusateur et humide" (*RF,* 67). This modern cyclops obviously bears little resemblance to the lawless, man-eating Polyphemus that threatened the lives of Odysseus and his men in *The Odyssey.* Indeed, it is as if the ancient myth had been consciously turned on its head, causing the soldiers (who are the modern counterparts for Odysseus' companions) to appear as the exemplary villains, waging war on even the most innocent of beasts. And whereas Polyphemus' eye has often been associated with vulnerability and simpleness, the horse's eye in *La Route des Flandres* reminds the men of their own ignorance of life: "comme si par delà la mort il nous narguait prophétique fort d'une connaissance d'une expérience que nous ne possédions pas, du décevant secret qu'est la certitude de l'absence de tout secret et de tout mystère" (*RF,* 270). For the horse's eye symbolizes a kind of ultimate knowledge about existence that is only revealed in the final hours before extinction; the terrified creature seems to belong more fittingly to Picasso's *Guernica* than to Homer's epic.

Simon's beast becomes the perfected model of man's exploitation of nature.   But the narrators recognize that there have also been thousands of others: "comme si déjà nous chevauchions leurs squelettes combien de chevaux combien de milliers de chevaux combien de dizaines la plage piétinée n'était plus qu'un enchevêtrement confus d'empreintes de sabots se superposant se détruisant" (*BF*, 34).   Ultimately, the famous horses of Don Quixote and Alexander, the stabled beast, and the decomposing horse that Georges discovers on the Flanders Road share a similar fate: "non plus viande boucanée et puante mais transmuée, assimilé par la terre profonde qui cache en elle sous sa chevelure d'herbe et de feuilles les ossements des défuntes Rossinantes et des défunts Bucéphales (et des défunts chevaliers, des défunts cochers de fiacre et des défunts Alexandres) retournés à l'état de chaux friable" (*RF*, 242).   Ironically enough, the fate of their masters parallels their own to such an extent that on the rubble-ridden Flanders Road, the remains of men, machines, horses, and children are virtually indistinguishable from one another.   Yet for Simon's narrators, the spilled blood of an injured horse alongside the road symbolizes something more than the ruins of war: it brutally reminds them of man's unjustifiable crimes against the very earth which gave him life: "comme s'il [le sang] sourdait non d'un animal, d'une simple bête abattue, mais d'une inexpiable et sacrilège blessure faite par les hommes (à la façon dont, dans les légendes, l'eau ou le vin jaillissent de la roche ou d'une montagne frappée d'un baton) au flanc argileux de la terre" (*RF*, 28).

The Guerrier

Camus' absurd hero, Sisyphus, labors to roll a rock up the mountainside, only to watch it slip back down again: "Sisyphe est le héros absurde.   Il l'est d'autant par son tourment.   Son mépris des dieux, sa haine de la mort et sa passion pour la vie, lui ont valu ce supplice indicible où tout l'être s'emploie à ne rien achever."[24]   He is tragic primarily because he is aware, conscious that his actions are but futile gestures: "il n'est pas de punition plus terrible que le travail inutile et sans espoir."[25]

So too, Simon's archetypal warrior becomes a sisyphistic victim of the war adventure, condemned to suffer repeatedly without understanding why: "c'était à présent une de ces créatures un de ces géants condamnés à d'impossibles travaux luttant arc-bouté nu musculeux et sans espoir non pas contre quelque monstre ou hydre ou chimère aux griffes de lion ou même quelque rocher un obstacle sur quoi il aurait au moins pu avoir une prise diriger ses forces mais contre quelque chose d'aussi insaisissable qu'un brouillard l'obscurité le vide" (*BP*, 63-64). Far worse than the allusions to Hercules' second labour with the nine-headed Hydra of Lerna, or Bellerophon's mighty contest with the three-headed Chimaera, cleverly engineered by his enemies, or even Sisyphus' futile struggle against the eternal rock, the plight of this modern warrior is markedly more hazardous and psychologically defeating, for he does not know who his enemies are or where they may be hiding. Reduced to a permanent state of paranoia, he trusts no one, not even his fellow soldiers:

> le regard à l'expression traquée empreint d'une conviction obtuse, furibonde, comme un défi permanent qui semblait adressé aussi bien à nous-mêmes qu'aux gradés et au monde entier, une permanente panique où le sentiment des injustices et des outrages subis engendrait, moins sans doute que la fureur vengeresse qu'il affichait, l'obsession lancinante de sa vulnérabilité et de cette nuée d'ennemis sans visages contre lesquels luttait en ce moment la blême et gigantesque nudité, gesticulant, le grand corps . . .comme une dérisoire parodie, une dérisoire réplique de tous les Persée, les Goliath, les Léonidas, la cohorte des guerriers figés dans les bitumeuses peintures des musées. . .
> (*BP*, 137)

This, then, is the modern rendition of the archetypal guerrier. And although decidedly less impressive than Perseus or Goliath, he somehow retains an unmistakable degree of heroic dignity: "auréolé de ce prestige particulier qui ne tient ni au grade ni à la valeur mais à la capacité de souffrance, au temps" (*BP*, 142). At base, he has the stuff of which heroes are made: endurance: "pitoyable maintenant, tragique, comme si en cachant sa nudité il avait en même temps abandonné, abdiqué cette dimension pour ainsi dire surnaturelle, fabuleuse, à laquelle elle le faisait accéder, et cependant toujours terrible, invaincu, invincible, comme hors d'atteinte, sourd aux ricanements étouffés. . .poursuivant sans doute dans les obscurs méandres de son cerveau ses rêves obscurs de révolte et de violence" (*BP*, 146). The image here of the soldier bared in front of his companions is both tragic and noble. It suggests that underneath the impressive armor and military garb, a man of dignity remains in wait, ready to revolt against all those who have unfairly wronged him. Even in his bleakest hours of suffering and ridicule, he is invincible. Yet in a very real sense, he can never *know* his enemies because the wrath and frenzy of modern warfare have assimilated virtually every man and nation into the deadly war-machine. The ancient wicked beast, which must be slain, is all around him and yet it is no where, due to its anonymity.

The narrator in *La Bataille de Pharsale* also refers to the archetypal warrior as Orion, an ancient mythological giant who was blinded by Oenopion, then obliged to move gropingly toward the sun, which alone could restore his sight: "dans l'avare lueur de la veilleuse éclairant la chambrée au milieu de laquelle ce Goliath ou plutôt cet Orion titubait en aveugle" (*BP*, 140). Here, as elsewhere, confusion and figurative blindness emerge as significant characteristics of the war experience. Soldiers wander aimlessly, because they have found no rational explanation for fratricide. In this context, Georges remembers the entire army on the Flanders Road as a blinded giant, moving without direction or reason: "tous les chevaux, les hommes, les wagons en train de piétiner ou de rouler en aveugles dans cette même nuit, cette même encre, sans savoir vers où ni vers quoi, le vieux et inusable monde tout entier frémissant" (*RF*, 33).

Both ancient and modern man have participated in the war effort and both have felt subjected to an incomprehensible power beyond themselves. For Simon's narrators, the history of war is a history of brandished arms and broken chains, of armies defeated, victorious, then defeated once again. Even the statues erected in public squares are an eternal reminder of man's continual frustrations and conflicts: "condamnés à se battre sans fin contre. . .contre. . ." (*BP*, 183). Like Sisyphus and Orion, the modern archetypal warrior belongs to that race of beings condemned to fight without any hope of lasting victory, without any hope of defeating the "invisible ennemi sans cesse vaincu et sans cesse réssuscitant" (*BP*, 241). In prison, he merely rechannels his aggression, lashing out at fellow companions with words, rather than swords or rifles: "comme quelque chose d'à la fois invisible et sale. . .pas de violence apparente pas de bras levés pas d'épées pas de javelines brandies mais comme on dit laver son linge sale comme dans ces drames de boulevard où dans l'atmosphère confinée d'un salon d'une chambre à coucher les personnages se portent des coups perfides s'assassinant par l'invisible moyen des paroles" (*BP*, 168). So it seems that Simon's narrators see little difference between the dilemma of ancient and modern conflict. If the enemy is never defeated, it is because the real enemy is man himself: "ce quelque chose d'invisible d'innommable d'impossible à atteindre à combattre sans forme l'intolérable en soi" (*BP*, 63).

Transformation

For the novice, each archetype encountered in the war experience becomes a universal symbol, illuminating the ultimate mysteries of his being and his world. It teaches him the order of his instincts, his dreams, and his thought.[26] Once exposed to the archetypal figures and the scenarios that accompany them, Simon's narrators begin their slow passage toward a new modality of being. Their transformation signifies both the end of innocence and the debacle of rationalism as the self becomes *other*.

Innocence is lost when the turmoil of war unleashes itself on the unsuspecting novice. What the narrators discover on the battlefield or in prison in no way corresponds to the tranquil, orderly universe of their elders: "où à travers les carreaux de verres de couleur le monde apparaissait unifié, fait d'une seule et même matière, verte, mauve ou bleue, enfin réconcilié" (*RF*, 243). Instead, war awakens them to a heretofore unknown world of cruelty, confusion, and filth: " 'je ne savais pas encore que des expressions comme marcher au feu le baptême du feu voir le feu n'étaient pas des métaphores armes à feu et que les traces que laisse la guerre derrière elle sont simplement noires et sales exactement comme la suie' " (*BP*, 111). Like their uniforms, once so new and immaculate, the narrators have been permanently blemished, we might even say ravaged, by the war experience. And, as the narrative voice observes in Simon's most recent novel, *Leçon de choses*, the unanticipated atrocities of war leave an unmistakable mark of premature disaster on the faces of young soldiers: "une barbe de cinq jours les fondent dans une sorte d'anonymat, comme si leur jeunesse avait été non pas exactement effacée mais pour ainsi dire si soudainement flétrie qu'ils évoquent ces adolescents frappés par quleque mal foudroyant, quelque brutale déchéance morale ou physique" (*LC*, 20).

The reason for an initial loss of innocence and resultant transformation in Simon's fiction are primarily determined by wartime incidents and appear to be threefold in nature. First, his narrators discover the horror of approaching death: "la sensation de mes viscères remontant, m'obstruant la gorge, la brûlure de mes vaisseaux dilatés, en même temps que la probable imminence de ma mort" (*BP*, 123), and acknowledge their own inevitable decomposition: "j'essayais de bouger gisant sous les décombres écrasé sous mon poids amas de granats de poutres mangées de vers me dévorant dans la boue marron du sommeil" (*HI*, 40). Second, they become increasingly indifferent to their own fate: "tuez-moi ne me tuez pas qu'est-ce que ça peut me je ne savais pas que la mort. . ." (*PB*, 86), or to the fate of others: "il y avait longtemps que j'avais cessé de m'intéresser—de pouvoir m'intéresser—à ce qui pouvait se passer sur le bord de la route" (*RF*, 17). Finally, they realize that war means chaos, a concept which defies any rational comprehension and one that must be experienced in order to be known: "quelque chose d'absolument contraire à ce que peut apprendre la pensée, de tellement éton-nant, de tellement. . ." (*RF*, 74).

Simon's narrators make use of imagery fusing soldiers with animals or with inanimate objects as a vehicle to convey this radical change in their mode of being. Each initiate's transforma-tion is dual in nature, affecting both his outer appearance and his inner spirit, or psychological state. Georges' own dehumaniza-tion in form and substance, while imprisoned in a "wagon à bestiaux," causes him to allude cynically to Ovid's great classic, *The Metamorphoses:*

'à moins que ce ne soit pas du tout une erreur et qu'on l'ait, conformément à l'usage pour lequel il [le wagon] a été construit, rempli de bestiaux, de sorte que nous serions devenus sans nous en rendre compte quelque chose comme des bêtes, il me semble que j'ai lu quelque part une histoire comme ça, des types métamorphosés d'un coup de baguette en cochons ou en arbres ou en cailloux, le tout par le moyen de vers latins. . .' pensant encore 'Comme quoi il n'a donc pas entièrement tort. Comme quoi somme toute les mots servent tout de même à quelque chose. . .Je lui dirai que j'avais déjà lu en latin ce qui m'est arrivé, ce qui fait que je n'ai pas été trop surprise et même dans une certaine mesure rassuré de savoir que ç'avait déjà été écrit, de sorte que tout l'argent qu'il a lui aussi dépensé pour me la faire apprendre n'aura pas été non plus complètement perdu.' (*RF*, 100)

Of course, Georges does not really believe that the Latin words read as a child prepared him for war, or love, or any other significant experience in life. Words evoke impressions of reality, but not reality itself. The more dehumanized Simon's narrators become, the more they recognize the futility of their own verbage to describe the irrational world that surrounds them: "des mots inventés dans l'espoir de rendre comestible—comme des pâtes vaguement sucrées sous lesquelles on dissimule aux enfants les médicaments amers—l'innommable réalité" (*RF*, 184).

As already noted, each narrator's transformation began with an initiatory rite of submission to the unknown arena of the battlefield, followed by suffering and discoveries which eventually led to a fundamental change in his existential condition. Donning the military uniform was, in fact, the inaugural event of this transformational process: "comme si la bouffissure de la décomposition s'était déjà par avance installée avait commencé son travail le jour où nous avions revêtu nos anonymes tenues de soldats, revêtant en même temps, comme une espèce de flétrissure, ce masque uniforme de fatigue de dégoût de crasse" (*RF*, 43). Like the animals man has domesticated for his own use and misuse, the uniformed soldiers resemble subjugated animals, clad with "dog tags" that bear witness to their bondage.

Combat further promotes their dehumanization. On the battlefield, the soldiers are reduced to either prey or predators. Thrown to the ground during an enemy attack, Georges attempts to move his immobilized body. When he finally leaves the war-torn area, he does so on all fours, like an animal cowering in fear and confusion: "réussissant à me mettre à quatre pattes la tête dans le prolongement du corps le visage dirigé vers la terre" (*RF*, 160-161). O. remembers an almost identical episode when he too was crouched on all fours: "le cheval couché sur le flanc moi-même à quatre pattes maintenant par terre en train d'essayer de savoir où étaient le haut et le bas ou même s'il y avait un haut et un bas et si j'avais encore des bras et des jambes c'est-à-dire si je pouvais encore me servir de mes bras et de mes jambes 'je ne souffrais pas' constatant seulement qu'ils me soutenaient plutôt à vrai dire à la façon d'une bête que d'un homme puisqu'il me fallait quatre points d'appui" (*BP*, 72-73). Hence the narrators learn that when threatened with imminent injury or death, an alarmed human being reacts much like a terrified animal. Panic-stricken, he sheds his rational modes of apprehension because he knows, either consciously or unconsciously, that they cannot protect him from a chance encounter with death. Georges observes such an incident when a man rushes out to warn him about a sniper. The man's body language relates his instinctual fear; he resembles a frightened crab out of water: "du haut de son cheval, l'ombre gesticulante faisant irruption hors d'une maison, courant vers eux sur la route à la façon d'un crabe. . . en train d'agiter incompréhensiblement ses deux pinces tandis que la voix lui parvenait d'un autre point, les mouvements et la voix semblant en quelque sorte séparés, dissociés. . .hurlant de nouveau, comme en proie à une sorte de colère désespérée. . ." (*RF*, 107-109). However, after continual exposure to suffering and death, soldiers and horses alike become indifferent to the fate of their fellow species. A natural instinct to survive, even at the expense of others clearly motivates both man and beast.

Once in prison, the soldiers are further stripped of their human characteristics. Even the enemy has been dehumanized: "le maréchal des logis. . .toujours pas un homme: quelque chose vraiment comme une sorte de homard, sous ses buffleteries, son casque, engoncé dans son manteau raide, les mains—ou plutôt les pinces—gantées de cuir luisant" (*BP*, 144). In addition, confinement in close quarters causes the prisoners to pace about like encaged animals: "comme si au-dessous du sommeil lui-même on pouvait continuer à percevoir cette espèce de constant malaise, de stérile et vaine agitation de bêtes en cage" (*RF*, 120). In no more than a year's time the captured soldiers have completely re-ordered their priorities for living: "en un an nous

avions appris à nous dépouiller non seulement de cet uniforme
. . .mais encore pour ainsi dire de notre peau. . .même plus des
soldats même plus des hommes, ayant peu à peu appris à être
quelque chose comme des animaux mangeant n'importe quand
et n'importe quoi" (*RF,* 290-291). Breathing, eating, and drink-
ing become their major preoccupations because these are the
most instinctive, most animal-like needs. Georges, for example,
identifies the faces of hungry soldiers gathering around a card
table with the looks of envious, starving wolves. The real torture,
however, is the mind, that uniquely human island of rationality
which never ceases to remind them that they are in fact men, not
animals. It is the same curse endured by Beckett's unnamable
narrator in *L'Innommable:*

> même pas des loups, c'est-à-dire affamés, et efflanqués,
> et hargneux, menaçants, mais affligés de cette faiblesse
> que ne connaissent pas les loups mais seulement les
> hommes, c'est-à-dire la raison, c'est-à-dire, au contraire
> de ce qui se fût passé s'ils eussent été de véritables loups,
> empêchés d'attaquer par la conscience de ce qui eût
> encouragé des loups à attaquer (leur nombre), découragés
> à l'avance par le calcul de ce qu'eussent représenté les
> quelques maigres galettes qu'ils convoitaient une fois
> partagées entre mille, restant donc là, se contentant de
> rôder, avec ces lueurs de meurtre dans leurs yeux. . . (*RF,*
> 172-173)

The final phase of dehumanization changes man from
animal to thing. This metamorphosis moves the human body
one step closer to its unavoidable death and disintegration.
Like the carcass of a dead animal, the seasoned prisoners have
become permanent hosts for parasites, but they no longer resist
their fate: "sentant avec indifférence grouiller sur leur corps la
vermine dont ils étaient couverts, les dizaines de minuscules poux
grisâtres dont ils avaient un jour découvert avec terreur le premier
. . .les laissant maintenant courir sur eux avec un sentiment de
permanent dégoût, de permanente impuissance et de permanente
décomposition" (*RF,* 216). The narrator in *Histoire* remembers
the face of a prisoner who was also subjected to this second level
of dehumanized transformation: "type que je devais voir plus
tard promené d'une baraque de prisonniers à l'autre tenu en
laisse par deux nègres une brique pendue à l'aide de fils de fer
sur sa poitrine avec l'écriteau J'ai volé le pain de mes camarades,

et non pas un visage humain mais une chose" (*III*, 61). Like the figures of Achilles, Crastinus, and the Mythological Cyclops, both the man-as-animals and man-as-object imagery reflect each narrator's constant obsession with man's impulse to destroy and his ultimate fate.

For Simon's narrators, the war experience constituted one of several journeys into the realm of the unknown. Their adventures are *archetypal* inasmuch as each narrator "has been able to battle past his personal and local historical limitations to the generally valid, normally human forms."[28] Their initiation, the archetypes discovered and assimilated en route, and their final transformation are all aspects of a symbolic, transhistorical dimension of experience, a dimension which is valid for all men. As such, their individual transformation merely parallels or repeats the standard metamorphoses undergone by men and women everywhere. By recording their thoughts, reveries, and memories, the narrators create a symbol-producing process that reveals the fundamental fantasies and instincts of all men in war, love, society, and nature. Human conflict is but one of the many irrational forces which periodically terrorize mankind. The archetypal horse conveyed this message at its death, but Georges was unable to decipher it until much later:

> ce permanent et inépuisable stock ou plutôt réservoir ou plutôt principe de toute violence et de toute passion qui semble errer imbécile désoeuvré et sans but à la surface de la terre comme ces vents ces typhons sans autre objet qu'une aveugle et nulle fureur sécouant sauvagement et au hasard ce qu'ils rencontrent sur leur chemin; maintenant peut-être avions-nous appris ce que savait ce cheval en train de mourir son oeil allongé velouté pensif doux et vide dans lequel je pouvais pourtant voir se refléter nos minuscules silhouettes, cet oeil du portrait ensanglante lui aussi allongé énigmatique et doux que j'interrogeais. . .
> (*RF*, 287-288)

Simon's narrators have thus learned that progress is illusory since the world is constantly on the verge of chaos: "à tout instant le monde ordonné et rassurant peut soudain chavirer, se retourner et se mettre sur le dos comme une vieille putain troussant ses jupes et, retournant au chaos originel, en dévoiler la face cachée pour montrer que son envers n'est qu'un simple entassement d'ordures et de détritus" (*HI*, 66-67). Given the precariousness of peace, the narrator in *Le Palace* cynically concludes that war periodically recurs not because of anything so comprehensible as hatred or material gain but merely because of habit; it seems that warfare, like the seasons of nature, is part of the natural cycle of human interaction: "parce qu'apparemment pour que cette vieille motte de terre et d'eau ne s'arrête pas de tourner lui faut-il sa périodique ration d'enfants écrasés sous des poutres, de femmes échevelées griffant leurs seins et de mains crispées sortant des gravats. . ." (*LP*, 127). Cognizant of these discoveries, Simon's characters humbly submit to an irrational power over which they have no control. Without question, the irrational forces at work in today's universe are as much a mystery for them as they were for primitive man in the archaic civilizations of long ago.

NOTES

[1]Michel Mansuy, "L'Imagination dans le nouveau roman" in *Nouveau Roman: hier, aujourd'hui,* ed. by J. Ricardou and F. Van Rossum-Guyon (Paris: UGE, 1972), Vol. I, p. 91.

[2]Joseph Campbell, *The Hero with a Thousand Faces* (1949; rept. New York: World, 1956), p. 101.

[3]Mircea Eliade, *Cosmos and History,* trans. by Willard R. Trask (1949; rpt. New York: Harper and Row, 1959), p. 34.

[4]Mircea Eliade, *Rites and Symbols of Initiation,* trans. by Willard R. Trask (1958; rpt. New York: Harper and Row, 1965), p. x.

[5]Joseph Campbell, *The Hero with a Thousand Faces,* p. 51.

[6]*Claude Simon: Analyse, Théorie.* Ed. by Jean Ricardou (Paris: UGE, 1975), p. 422.

[7]In a series of remarks addressed to Ludovic Janvier, Simon differentiates between real and described objects or events: "l'écriture ne peut prétendre, pour reprendre les termes dont vous vous servez, ni à 'redoubler' l'histoire déjà vécue, ni à la 'sauver,' ni à lui 'offrir un terme,' mais à *dire* une histoire qui, encore une fois, n'entretient avec l'histoire 'déjà vécue' que les très rélatifs rapports de la pomme peinte avec la pomme 'réelle,' " in *Entretiens: Claude Simon,* ed. by M. Séguier (Toulouse: Subervie, 1972), p. 23.

[8]Roquentin experiences "une sorte de nausée dans les mains" when the pebble he holds in his hand loses its familiar solidity and seems to come alive: "les objets, cela ne devrait pas 'toucher,' puisque cela ne vit pas. . . Et moi, ils me touchent, c'est insupportable. J'ai peur d'entrer en contact avec eux tout comme s'ils étaient des bêtes vivantes." See Jean-Paul Sartre, *La Nausée* (Paris: Gallimard, 1938), p. 22.

[9]Mircea Eliade, *Rites and Symbols of Initiation,* p. 128.

[10]Mircea Eliade, *Images and Symbols,* trans. by Willard R. Trask (1952; rpt. New York: Sheed and Ward, 1969), p. 57.

[11]The Flanders Road (more often referred to as the Spanish Road), has been the historical setting for numerous European battles. Located near the French-Belgian border, it was one of the many battle sites during the 100 Years War between France and England, the disputes involving the Spanish Netherlands in the 30 Years War, the French Revolutionary conquest in 1794, and the early fighting of World War II.

[12]Jean Ricardou, *Problèmes du nouveau roman* (Paris: Seuil, 1967), p. 134.

[13]The ambiguity of the narrator's thought process in this brief passage suggests that "le sort du monde" is also the spectacle of love during which time the male sexual organ moves like the sword in war. In Simon's novels, war and love are similar to the extent that they both result in violence and death. War brings about a definitive end to life, whereas love-making culminates in a momentary death-like experience. Both violence and death in love are discussed at some length in the next chapter on The Archetypal Feminine.

[14]Mircea Eliade, *Cosmos and History,* p. 89.

[15]Georges Gusdorf, *Mythe et métaphysique* (Paris: Flammarion, 1953), p. 30.

[16]T. S. Eliot, "Ulysses, Order and Myth" in *The Dial* LXXV (1923), p. 483. See Lillian Feder, *Ancient Myth in Modern Poetry* (Princeton: Princeton University Press, 1971), p. 26.

[17]Joseph Campbell, *The Hero with a Thousand Faces,* p. 238.

[18]*Ibid.,* p. 55.

[19]Gilles Deleuze, *Proust et les signes* (Paris: PUF, 1971), p. 8.

[20]In the second and third lines, Valéry refers to Zeno's argument about flight. At each moment of its journey, the arrow presumably corresponds with an immobile line and therefore cannot actually move. The last two lines of the stanza refer to yet another paradox concerning Achilles

and the tortoise. Achilles moves twice as fast as the tortoise, who begins the race ten yards ahead of him. Achilles never beats the tortoise because for each distance he travels, the tortoise travels half again as much and always remains in front of him.

[21]J. Burnet, *Early Greek Philosophy* (1930), p. 182. Consult Paul Valéry, *Le Cimetière marin*, ed. by Graham Dunstan Martin (Austin: University of Texas Press, 1972), p. 59.

[22]This stanza has puzzled more than one contemporary critic. For a variety of interpretations consult: Gustave Cohen, *Essai d'explication du cimetière marin* (Paris: Gallimard and De Visscher, 1946); Bernard Weinberg, *The Limits of Symbolism* (Chicago: Chicago University Press, 1966); and Graham Dustan Martin's recent edition and translation: Paul Valéry, *Le Cimetière marin.*

[23]Martin, p. 60.

[24]Albert Camus, *Le Mythe de Sisyphe* (Paris: Gallimard, 1942), p. 162.

[25]*Ibid.*, p. 161.

[26]Joseph Campbell, *The Masks of God: Creative Mythology* (New York: Viking, 1971), p. 677.

[27]The Unnamable would like to return to his earliest "sensational" existence as "Worm," but is forever plagued by his subsequent "rational" existence as "Mahood." Worm and Mahood function as polar opposites in *L'Innommable*, representing the most primitive and the most complex modes of consciousness. See Samuel Beckett, *L'Innommable* (Paris: Minuit, 1953).

[28]Joseph Campbell, *The Hero with a Thousand Faces*, pp. 19-20.

II

THE ARCHETYPAL FEMININE

Sexual intimacy and the feminine mystique, like aggression and man's awareness of death, are also construed as perennial forces that dominate a principal segment of human experience in Simon's fiction. As such, they too are portrayed in archetypal or mythological terms. Reminiscing or fantasizing about their pasts, his narrators uncover the goals of their sexual drives, as well as the obstacles to be confronted, through the archetypal roles of the female and the revelations made in her presence. Primarily, woman functions as each narrator's *guide* to sensual and erotic adventures. Furthermore, they associate her with the principal aspects of the life process: nutrition, passion, aggression, and death. But above all, the archetypal woman is an enigma, symbolizing the undecipherable, feminine side of life that continually beckons but never satiates the male pursuer.

Rejecting Freud's ideology of "pure sexuality," Eliade argues "that sexuality never has been 'pure,' that everywhere and always it is a polyvalent function whose primary and perhaps supreme valency is the cosmological function. . .except in the modern world, sexuality has everywhere and always been a *hierophany*, and the sexual act an integral action (therefore also a means to knowledge)."[1] Likewise, woman functions as a supreme *hierophant* for Simon's narrators, that is, an enchanting guide and interpreter of the sacred mysteries of life. Hence to know her is to know the mystifying other half of being in the world. As a submitting partner, she enables the narrators to discover man's inner craving for sensuality, eroticism, and the eternal.[2] Through their encounters with her, they attempt to recapture: 1) the blissful experience of the primal condition, when infant and mother were one, and 2) the animal-like frenzy and oblivion found in erotic union. Yet because the narrators never fully comprehend her being, woman is also "directement associée à l'échec,"[3] for she remains an eternal mystery, evoking both their reverence and contempt.

The Good Mother

A symbolic dispenser of life and pleasure, woman invites Simon's narrators to experience the fullness of her physical being. As an archetypal mother, she offers them the nourishment, warmth, and security found in the natural world. Her maternal womb represents the womb of the unconscious where man loses his ego and, in so doing, is reunited with the formlessness of the liquid world. Hence, like the warriors discussed earlier, the qualities of woman are universal rather than individual: "non pas une enfant, ou une jeune femme, ou une vieille femme, mais une femme sans âge, comme une addition de toutes les femmes" (*RF*, 148).

For the narrators, woman becomes synonymous with the sustaining life forces. Metaphorically speaking, their most prominent sensual imagery associates woman with milk or water. The prevalence of liquid imagery in Simon's texts is in many ways a psychologically revealing practice since it appears to be intimately related to the role of woman as a maternal figure, the provider of a primal liquid that is both warm and nourishing. Thus, after a fleeting glimpse of a young farm woman, Georges feels her warmth welling up inside him:

> une chose tiède, blanche comme le lait qu'elle venait de tirer au moment où ils étaient arrivés, une sorte d'apparition non pas éclairée par cette lampe mais luminescente, comme si sa peau était elle-même la source de la lumière, comme si toute cette interminable chevauchée nocturne n'avait eu d'autre raison, d'autre but que la découverte à la fin de cette chair diaphane modelée dans l'épaisseur de la nuit: non pas une femme mais l'idée même, le symbole de toute femme. . . (*RF*, 41)

The triade of woman/liquid/light in the passage above has a surprisingly mystical quality, endowing the common image of maternal milk with a status bordering on the revered or sacred. Elsewhere, the frequent use of verbs like "se nourrirait," "buvant," "suçant," "me désaltérer," emphasizes the importance given to woman's role as an affectionate provider. In addition, these verbs and others suggest that Simon's narrators acknowledge their primary relation to woman as one of *dependence* for their psychic and biological survival, a dependence modeled on the primal love of the child for its mother.[4]

The association of woman and milk is further complicated in the narrators' minds with the added suggestion that milk flows not only from woman's mammary glands, but from her entire body, whose blue-white color reminds them of the primal liquid. O., the narrator in *La Bataille de Pharsale*, remembers his movements toward a woman whose kimono is covered with sensually stimulating images from nature. However, the most evocative image clearly refers to her milk-like body: "j'écartais les fleurs les hérons découvrant cette comment dire laiteuse lait plus blanc que le blanc bleuâtre à force d'être blanc avec des ombres d'un vert léger jade courant sur la peau transparente me désaltérer" (*BP, 47*). Images connecting woman to milk also allude to the fragile nature of her being. Leaving the barn, Georges' farm woman virtually *melts away* into the night: "sa silhouette se découpant un instant en sombre tant qu'elle fut dans la pénombre de la grange, puis, sitôt le seuil franchi, semblant s'évanouir, quoiqu'ils continuassent à la suivre des yeux non pas s'éloignant mais, aurait-on dit, se dissolvant, se fondant" (*RF, 39*). Almost transparent in the light, she seems as unreal as an apparition. Indeed, her liquid body attracts man's touch, but appears intangible as if it might dissolve with the slightest contact.

In all three novels, Corinne, the infamous cousin, haunts the narrators with her alluring body and fickle nature and, although markedly aging in *Triptyque,* still retains and exploits her curiously captivating charm. So important is her role in Simon's narrative odysseys that she actually becomes one of the two or three primary structural focal points in *La Route des Flandres.* The entire novel surveys Georges' fluctuating thoughts and memories while in bed with her. Like other women in Simon's fiction, Corinne becomes a symbolic mother for her lovers, despite or perhaps because of the fact that she has no children of her own: "elle qui n'avait jamais allaité désaltéré été bue par d'autres que des rudes lèvres d'homme: au centre il y avait on pouvait deviner comme une minuscule fente horizontale aux bords collés d'où pourrait couler d'où jaillissait invisible le lait de l'oubli" (*RF*, 261). For the archetyapl mother, man himself is her infant. And it is from her sexual organ that he drinks the milk of oblivion.

Georges rediscovers an infant-like dependency and security while drinking from her body. The sense of separateness pervading his adult life is momentarily suspended as he re-experiences the protected existence of the foetus: "il ne restait plus alors de mon corps qu'un foetus ratatiné rapetissé couché entre les lèvres du fossé comme si je pouvais m'y fondre y disparaître m'y engloutir accroché comme ces petits singes sous le ventre de leur mère à ses seins multiples m'enfoussant dans cette moiteur fauve" (*RF*, 257). The imagery in the above quotation exemplifies Freud's theory, restated by Norman O. Brown, that the child's initial experience of love for the mother "stays with us as the immortal dream of love, as an indestructible demand of human nature, as the source of our restless discontent. The infantile experience to which our dreams return is an experience of pleasure, so that a return to the pleasure-principle is an indestructible demand of human nature."[5] For this reason, man's struggle to recapture the nourishing union of mother and child has no temporal or cultural boundaries in Simon's fiction. Pointing out the mythic proportions of his desire for the farm woman, Georges associates himself and others to the descendants of Atreus, the ancient king of Mycenae: "nous n'étions pas dans la boue de l'automne nous n'étions nulle part mille ans ou deux mille ans plus tôt ou plus tard en plein dans la folie le meurtre les Atrides, chevauchant à travers le temps la nuit ruisselante de pluie sur nos bêtes fourbues pour parvenir jusqu'à elle la découvrir la trouver tiède demi nue et laiteuse dans cette écurie à la lueur de cette lanterne" (*RF*, 122). Once again the triade of woman/liquid/light dominates the passage, but this time it is set-off even more fully as a desirable end when counterbalanced with soldiers/rain-mud/night. By contrasting a sexually awakened Louis in white with a dying, sexless Marie in black, the text of *L'Herbe* also indicates that the color white is the very essence of *presence*, while black connotes a condition of *absence* (*HE*, 27).

Because woman is perceived as a dispenser of the life force, she is also associated with water and earth, two of the most obvious life-producing elements in the natural world. In *Histoire,* the narrator remembers how Corinne and Hélène, his ex-wife, were in love with the sea. Even as a young child, Corinne is linked to the sensuality and comfort of the sea with her "tête d'ange aux cheveux mouillés" (*HI,* 233). On a more complex imagistic level, Corinne and Hélène become symbols for both the sea and the life produced in it. Thus, Georges imagines Corinne's body as a delicate madrepore: "comme si elle était faite d'une matière semblable à celle des éponges, mais d'un grain invisible, se dilatant et se contractant, semblable à ces fleurs, ces choses marines à mi-chemin entre le végétal et l'animal, ces madrépores, palpitant delicatement dans l'eau transparente" (*RF,* 236). Corinne's attraction lies in her ambiguous nature, which is located halfway between the animal and vegetable kingdoms. Returning from a swim, Hélène's slender, fish-like body also tastes and smells of the salty sea (*HI,* 322). Such woman-fish imagery is sexually stimulating in the minds of Simon's narrators because it emphasizes the fish's slippery movement and liquid world which simultaneously evokes an atmosphere of sweating bodies and ejaculated semen.

However, the metaphor of woman-fish is also reversed on occasion to accomodate the more usual association of fish and the male sexual organ, which becomes an image of recurrent fascination for the young adolescents as well as the narrative consciousness in *Triptyque.* In *La Route des Flandres,* Georges imagines his own sexual organ as a fish that cannot survive without its subterranean cavern, the female vagina: "comme ceux de ces animaux poissons qui vivent dans les rivières souterraines les cavernes, devenus aveugles à force d'habiter les ténèbres bouche et oeil suppliants et furibonds de carpe ou quoi apoplectique hors de l'eau exigeant suppliant de retourner aux humides et secrètes cachettes, la bouche d'ombre" (*RF,* 290). Woman penetrated thereby signifies a descent into the other world of the liquid womb-cave, the mysterious receptacle from whence each man is born. Likewise, the birth of human history presumably began in paleolithic caves, the wombs of Mother Nature. Like the protected darkness of distant sea caverns, the reassuring, shadowy depths of the female vagina grant security and nourishment amid the turmoil and pain of adult existence.

As an earth symbol, the female body represents the immobility found in the earth after death. In bed, her rounded form exhales "la senteur immobile de la terre" (*HI*, 382). In a similar fashion, Louise, the female protagonist in *L'Herbe*, acutely senses her own sexuality mingled with a death wish when lying on the ground, as if she were part of the earth's deepest center. Remembering the war, O.'s thoughts in *La Bataille de Pharsale* turn suddenly to woman: like the earth during battle, she becomes an attractive refuge from life's burdens: " 'ne souffrais pas' toujours à quatre pattes lourd comme si la terre m'aspirait ma tête tirée vers le bas le sol l'odeur d'humus de mousse je pesais mille kilos tonnes de pierre de marbre de bronze je m'écrasai elle ecarta encore ses cuisses je sentis ses bras minces m'entourer les reins m'agripper le bracelet s'enfonçant dans ma peau" (*BP*, 75). Performing her role as soothing mother, she deafens man's ears to the turbulent activities outside with the silent depths of her body: "comme si peu à peu le ciment de silence se refermait sur lui l'engloutissait espèce de ciment noir dans le nez aussi les poumons pleins de terre immobile déjà se vidant et se remplissant de terre" (*HI*, 383). Here, as elsewhere, the death wish mingles with the desire for fusion. The persistent association in the Simonian text of the maternal vagina-*womb* and the earthy *tomb* is psychically revealing, for woman and earth both offer silence and immobility.

As a rule, Simon's narrators reach out to woman for sustenance like a defenseless infant in need of its protective womb. Nestling in her warmth, they attempt to forget the horrors discovered in a universe governed by the irrationality of chance and the constancy of change. In the meanderings of each narrative consciousness, the feminine species often approximates Erich Neumann's archetypal Good Mother, "mankind's instinctive experience of the world's depth and beauty, of the goodness and graciousness of Mother Nature."[6] To be sure, the image of the Good Mother means several things at once, for while it signifies a desire for protection and nourishment, it also stresses the "desire to re-enter into the bliss of living matter that is still 'unformed,' with all its possible lines of development, cosmological, anthropological, etc."[7]

However, the aim of each narrator's Eros is ultimately union with an object outside himself. Yet childlike dependency and passivity hinder his attempts to merge on an equal footing with a separate individual. Woman consoles him with her all-encompassing warmth, but cannot satiate him in her role as nourishing, protecting mother. Only complete physical fusion offers satisfaction, but in a Simonian context this involves mutual acts of bestiality and frenzy. For a more fulfilling union, passivity must therefore yeild to violence and simulated death for both partners.

Erotic Partners

A second, complementary female role emerges from the narrator's memories and fantasies in the form of a voluptuous sexual partner. And like the mother figure, she too appeals to their instinctual, rather than intellectual, leanings. The predominance of animal and mythological imagery to describe this additional feminine form affirms the profoundly erotic nature of the male-female encounter.[8] For it is, in fact, primarily through erotic behavior and fantasies that Simon's narrators strive to destroy the self-contained quality of their existence by merging with another in an exuberant celebration of life. Hence they no longer cling solely to a nurturing mother figure, but aggressively seek to initiate and complete a physical union. To attain this union, however, they must first seek the presence of a desirable object.

As noted earlier, liquid imagery in association with woman establishes her ethereal as well as her protective qualities. Yet at the same time, each narrator's prolific use of animal and mythological imagery contradicts this ethereal nature. Herein lies the erotic value of the feminine form. Bataille argues that "the image of the desirable woman as first imagined [ethereal] would be insipid and unprovocative if it did not at the same time also promise or reveal a mysterious animal aspect, more momentously suggestive."[9] The attraction once again stems from woman's ambiguous nature. Intrigued by her contradictions, Georges carefully reconstructs Iglésia's description of Corinne as one of the fabulous beings: "d'une nature hybride, ambiguë, pas tout à fait humains, pas tout à fait objets, inspirant à la fois le respect et l'irrespect par la rencontre, la réunion en eux d'éléments composants (réels ou supposés) disparates—humains et inhumains —" (*RF*, 141). To penetrate the female is therefore equivalent to

an exploration of the ambiguities of life, an investigation of all
that is contradictory and incomprehensible in the world outside
as well as inside the vagina.

Leda and the Peacock

The narrators associate themselves and women with various
animals, among which the bird, dog, and horse are the most
prominent.   Each animal represents a different aspect of the
female character, evoking a complementary and instinctual re-
sponse from the narrator.   The animal imagery is then often
linked to mythological imagery, suggesting the timelessness of
erotic behavior.   Above all, erotic union is first and foremost a
union of fleshy bodies, not of minds.

Bird images often stress woman's delicacy and flighty
intangibility while in the male presence.   The peacock imagery
in *La Route des Flandres,* for instance, is a prime example.
Georges associates the aforementioned anonymous farm woman
with the captivating peacock printed on her curtains.   Like the
woman living behind it, the mysterious peacock coyly beckons
him with its "queue chamarée d'yeux se balaçant oscillant
mystérieux" (*RF,* 263).   Irritated with her secrets and continued
aloofness, Georges wonders: "de qui donc le paon de quelle
divinité est-il l'oiseau vaniteux fat stupide promenant solennel
ses plumes multicolores sur les pelouses des châteaux et les
coussins des concierges?" (*RF,* 289).   Obviously, he refers here
to the peacock's traditional role as a symbol for the aristocra-
cy.[10]   The peacock was also the favorite bird of Hera, the wife
of Zeus.

Because fusion with the farm woman is his final goal,
Georges becomes decidedly annoyed by the bird's snobbish
appearance and mannerisms: "(mais Georges ne regardait plus,
épiait seulement avec avidité le filet d'un blanc grisâtre mainten-
ant immobile et où le décoratif et prétentieux oiseau se tenait
coi derrière l'impalpable bruine qui continuait à tomber, silencie-
use, patiente, éternelle)" (*RF,* 62).   Although direct physical
contact with the peacock-woman never occurs, the image never-

theless retains a strong esthetic appeal. So that later, as the same narrator touches Corinne, she too takes on the physical attributes of a delicate, quivering bird: "il éprouva d'abord la bizarre sensation de ne pas la toucher vraiment, comme lorsqu'on prend un oiseau dans la main: cette surprise, cet étonnement provoqué par la différence entre le volume apparant et le poids réel, l'incroyable légereté, l'incroyable délicatesse, la tragique fragilité des plumes, du duvet" (*RF*, 238). Through archetypal and mythological imagery, Corinne, like Hélène and the farm woman, is subject to continued depersonalization. In so doing, the narrators connect her ostensibly incidental characteristics with the more universal patterns of feminine appearance and conduct. Hence they regard her as a model representative of her sex and her delicate, bird-like skin as that of the eternally seductive female: "telle est, pensa-t-il, l'exquise délicatesse de la chair des femmes qu'on hésite à croire qu'on les touche réellement, la chair toute entière comme des plumes, de l'herbe, des feuilles, de l'air transparent, aussi fragile que du cristal" (*RF*, 243).

Georges' furtive attempts to hold and possess Corinne illustrate man's endless need to capture an alluring female partner. With his use of specific mythological references, we enter what Campbell terms "the sphere of dream awake," where the actions and desires may appear on one level local, personal, and historic, but in fact, are rooted in the instincts of the species.[11] In bed with Corinne, Georges likens her to a swan, then associates the swan to the lovely Leda in Greek mythology: "quittant mon cou son autre bras semblait ramper le long d'elle-même comme un animal comme un col de cygne invertébré se faufilant le long de la hanche de Léda" (*RF*, 262). According to the ancient myths, Leda was the beautiful daughter of King Thestius who gave her in marriage to Tyndareus, King of Sparta. Enamored with Leda, Zeus visited her in the form of a swan. She later gave birth to Pollux and Helen, children of Zeus. In the previous quotation, however, Corinne alternately becomes both the lover and the beloved when referred to first as the swan and then as Leda. Thus, from an historical viewpoint, Georges' image is actually misleading since the reader may have the impression that Leda and the swan are one and the same. Yet, bearing in mind the Greek story, Georges' interpretation or what we might better term *re-creation*, of the myth is of interest because it accentuates the female's narcissistic nature. For the narrator, Corinne represents both Leda and the swan as she strokes her own body. Ambiguous as always, she is simultaneously the captivating woman and the lustful god disguised as beast. Like Simon's other narrators, Georges seems more fascinated with the mental image of these mythological figures than with the specifics of their traditional story since his primary concern is to provoke the sensuous immediacy of his own experiences.

The Matron and Pasiphae

Despite associations with Zeus, however, bird images remain the least bestial of animal images throughout the three novels. For while the narrators commonly link young women to delicate birds, their more erotic images relate mature females to four-legged animals like the dog, ass, bull, and horse. Georges makes this distinction clear when describing the women gathered at the horse races as physically comparable to young delicate fillies until they reach their mid-thirties, at which time the women take on a more masculine, as well as more mature, horse-like appearance (*RF*, 19). With age, the narrator suggests, women become increasingly corpulent and, as a consequence, more awakened to the sexual desires of their own fleshy bodies.

The narrators' canine associations deal with the mouth or tongue as the focus of erotic desire and activity. Georges mentions his need to lick the farm woman and his pavlovian reflex of salivation while imagining Corinne's naked body. Later, Georges completes the analogy in his mind when he and Corinne are transformed into mad, galloping dogs during their physical encounter (*RF*, 291). And since the mental image of the canine tongue arouses his physical excitement, Georges also compares Corinne's sexual organs to a dog's tongue: "comme la langue d'un petit chien frétillant jappant de plaisir" (*RF*, 292). Pounding on the door, the narrator in *La Bataille de Pharsale* senses that the woman he loves is in the company of another man. He too pictures them as a pair of frightened dogs, immobilized by his presence: "pilon rouge entrant et sortant immobilisés soudain dans la posture encore à demi enfoncé peut-être n'osant plus respirer chiens collés la sueur refroidissant sur leurs corps nus" (*BP*, 57). For both Georges and O., the use of dog imagery suggests a rejection of sexual sublimation and a promotion of the instinctual reality within man and woman. Thus, the two narrators embrace both Nietzsche's drunken Dionysus, who calls our entire body symbolism into the foreground, and Freud's conception of the *id*, which he termed "a chaos, a cauldron of seething excitement."[12]

Woman-horse images abound in Simon's fiction. In *La Route des Flandres*, Georges refers to Corinne time and again as "l'alezane-femme, la blonde femelle" (*RF*, 185). Haunted by the image of Corinne and Iglésia making love in the horse stables, Georges visualizes Iglésia as a bird of prey on a golden horse: "ses petites jambes repliées, les genoux remontés, accroupi sur cette alezane dorée à la démarche majestueuse, opulente, aux hanches opulentes" (*RF*, 24). In addition, Simon's narrators usually correlate horseback riding with erotic activity. O. remembers the straddle of his body position during love-making: "comme s'il chevauchait un invisible cheval" (*BP*, 244). Indeed, the present participle "chevauchant" becomes definitively linked with eroticism in *La Route des Flandres*. Georges' rhythmic word associations evoke the physical movements of a horse as the two human bodies are transformed into one single equine beast: "c'était elle qui écartait les cuisses chevauchait, tous deux chevauchant (ou plutôt qui avaient été chevauchés par) la même houri la même haletante hoquetante haquenée, avançant donc dans le paisible et éblouissant après-midi" (*RF*, 296). By utilizing animal imagery in this fashion, Simon's narrators express their mythic understanding of human sexuality. "Le mythe," asserts Gusdorf, "connaît et reconnaît la différence des sexes, ainsi que leur quête d'unité. La sexualité est l'un des centres d'intérêt capitaux de la conscience mythique."[13] Animal imagery in the Simonian text emphasizes the aggressive tendencies embedded in human nature, while mythological references stress the timelessness of the erotic couple since the phsyical desires of ancient mythological figures accord so convincingly with those of contemporary people: "pensant à tous les corps d'hommes et de femmes accolés haletants" (*HI*, 370). With repeated references to the Greco-latin myth recounted in *The Golden Ass*, Simon's narrators continue to underline this transtemporal correspondence.

In *La Route des Flandres*, *Histoire*, and *La Bataille de*

Pharsale the narrators relate dog or horse images to an erotic episode from Apuleius' classic, *The Golden Ass,* described as "The preposterous adventures of a young voluptuary who partakes of a magic potion and is transformed into an Ass."[14] In every instance, the narrators refer to a specific incident in which Lucius (the protagonist), transformed into an ass, becomes intimate with a married woman who has fallen in love with him. Lying in bed with Corinne, who was his captain's wife, Georges takes on the characteristics of this same mythological beast whose animal body and human soul brought the matron such great pleasure: "je n'étais plus un homme mais un animal un chien plus qu'un homme une bête si je pouvais y atteindre connaître l'âne d'Apulée poussant sans trêve en elle fondant maintenant ouverte comme un fruit une pêche jusqu'à ce que ma nuque éclate" (*RF*, 292). As an exemplary erotic partner, Corinne helps Georges move closer to an ideal synthesis of man and beast, which, for him, is embodied in the figure of the golden ass, symbolizing the acme of erotic pleasure.

The similarity perceived by man in ancient times between the human act of love and bestiality is also acknowledged in *Histoire.* Recalling his affair with Corinne many times, the narrator remembers one instance in particular in the woods, imagining her as a horse and himself as the half-man-half-animal creature who rode her. Here again, the narrator couples his erotic experiences in love with the ancient myth recorded in Apuleius' tale:

> Se faire baiser ou plutôt cette fois se faire monter par Imaginant quelque chose de faunesque quelque chose avec de l'herbe des feuillages (peut-être à cause des champs de course des haies) et pas un homme mais une sorte de créature hybride aussi moitié étalon moitié homme s'avançant en sautillant maladroitement à la façon d'un caniche debout sur ses pattes de derrière ses bottes. . . l'âne d'Apulée copuler moi vaguement écoeuré. . . (*HI*, 341-342)

Referring to this same myth, the narrator in *La Bataille de Pharsale* quotes from Book 10 of *The Golden Ass.* The passage is in italics, indicating that it is indeed a direct quote:[15]

'comment avec de si grosses et si longues pattes pourrais-

je chevaucher un corps si délicat comment avec mes durs
sabots étreindre des membres si blancs si tendres faits de
lait et de miel. . .et elle pendant ce temps multipliait les
mots tendres ses furieux baisers ses doux gémissements
ses yeux me mordaient Je te tiens me dit-elle dans un
paroxysme je tiens mon petit pigeon mon passereau et
alors combien mes imaginations avaient été fausses et
mes craintee stupides elle me le prouva. . .saisissant ma
pine à pleines mains elle l'enfonçait dans une étreinte
encore plus profonde si bien que Hércule! j'aurais même
pu croire que pour la faire jouir complètement il me
manquait encore quelque chose ah! que la mère du
Minotaure et son mugissant amant' (*BP*, 93)

What we have here, then, is not only a highly suggestive passage
from Latin mythology but, at the same time, a total role re-
versal in the feminine partner. Lucius, like O. in *La Bataille de
Pharsale,* is reticent to penetrate the delicate woman who desires
him. Yet, as the passage progresses, it becomes more and more
apparent that it is the woman who is unharnessing an extremely
powerful sexual drive. The mounting of her frenzy is sharply
delineated by the continued escalation of her physically arousing
acts, demonstrated by such passages as: "en feu jusqu'au bout
des ongles," "ses yeux me mordaient," "m'embrassant plus
étroitement encore," "elle se rapprochait avec frénésie," and
"dans une étreinte encore plus profonde." Clearly, she is no
longer perceived as the dainty bird-like creature in aforemen-
tioned passages. On the contrary, if either of the two lovers is
sexually possessed by the other, it is surely Lucius himself who is
held by the matron, for she refers to him as "mon petit pigeon
mon passereau." At the apex of sexual excitement, Lucius even
wonders whether he will be able to satisfy her sexual hunger.
The fact that his partner is older, married, and obviously cogni-
zant of her own sexual needs, underscores the significant role of
woman as an experienced guide to erotic pleasure and ecstasy
for both Lucius and for Simon's narrator.

In the last lines of this passage from *The Golden Ass,* Lucius
recognizes the similarities between their own situation and that
of another well-known Greek couple: Pasiphae and her bull
lover. Earlier, in Harry Schnur's translation of the Latin passage,
Lucius first associates the rich matron to Pasiphae while speaking
of her "passions and disordinate appetite." He recalls how the

young woman "continually desired to have her pleasure with me, like a new Pasiphae, but with an ass."[16]   According to Greek mythology, King Minos of Crete was in need of Poseidon's help so he prayed for a bull to appear from the sea which he might then sacrifice to Poseidon.   In some versions of the myth, the bull came forth, but was so handsome that Minos refused to kill it.   In other accounts, Minos sacrificed his best bull yearly, but one year chose an inferior bull.   But in both versions, Pasiphae was fated to fall in love with the bull that had not been sacrificed.   Eventually, she gave birth to the Minotaur, which Minos hid in the Labyrinth.   Pasiphae, then, was the second in her family to fall victim to a bull-lover for Zeus had previously seduced Europa, the mother of Minos, by transforming himself into a bull.

The use of the quote from Apuleius in *La Bataille de Pharsale* creates a mirrored perspective, as O. compares himself to Lucius, who in turn compares himself to the handsome bull. The passage thereby becomes *mythic* in the broadest sense of the word: "le mythe désigne un régime de l'existence caracterisé par le fait que ses structures ont une validité permanente, non pas historique, pourrait-on dire mas ontologique."[17]   Time is momentarily suspended, as separate couples from three temporally distinct civilizations merge, forming an archetypal couple. There is, in fact, considerable evidence to suggest that the image of the bull continues to function as the male symbol of fertility and sexual prowess in the modern psyche. In Simon's novels, mental images often extend beyond the realm of the personal because his narrators are invariably reminded of analogous situations in history, in the lives of others, or in the surrounding environment. From their pasts, they bring forth certain underlying similarities which constitute the general human experience. Time passes, civilizations emerge and perish, but the archetypal couple still rises up from the earth's depths like the spirited mythological giants of antiquity:

> tous deux semblables à quelque divinité bicéphale, de noirs héros sortis de quelque fabuleuse gigantomachie, comme des jumeaux mythologiques jaillis jusqu'à mi-corps d'une blessure de la terre, venus tout droit, avec leurs yeux sombres, leurs corps d'anthracite, leur impitoyable capacité de souffrance. . .dominant de toute leur hauteur la vieille boule ridée, marquetée, mosaïquée

de mers, d'océans, de mystérieux continents, tournoyant lentement dans les ténèbres. . . (*HI*, 126)

Taboo, Transgression, and Death

Their obvious bestiality aside, the three mythological couples mentioned in the preceding section contribute a strong element of guilt to their love-making sessions, which doubly enhances the erotic appeal of their encounters. Leda, Pasiphae, and the wealthy matron in *The Golden Ass* all legitimately belong to their husbands, but secretly give themselves to animal-like creatures. The concepts of taboo and transgression are therefore readily applicable in each case, concepts relating to Bataille's understanding of eroticism, for it can happen, he reminds us, "that unless we see that transgression is taking place we no longer have the feeling of freedom that the full accomplishment of the sexual act demands,—so much so that a scabrous situation is sometimes necessary to a blasé individual for him to reach the peak of enjoyment (or if not the situation itself, an imaginary one lived out like a daydream during intercourse)."[18] The broken taboos that form the bases of the archetypal relationships examined in the three novels thus far are surely not coincidental since, as in Proust's own masterpiece, the theme of infidelity runs throughout virtually all of Simon's work: in *Le Sacre du printemps*, Bernard is crushed when he discovers that the girl he idealized has been sexually active and is pregnant, Louise, the young married protagonist of *L'Herbe*, meets her lover secretly in the fields but worries about her infidelity, the nephew in *Histoire* laments Hélène's inconstant heart, O. is haunted by his lover's betrayal in *La Bataille de Pharsale*, the drunken newlywed husband in *Triptyque* sleeps with his former girlfriend and then returns to a tearful bride, and images of Corinne deceiving her husband permeate *La Route des Flandres* and appear in *Histoire* and *La Bataille de Pharsale* as well.

In a recent essay on "Les Signes de l'Eros," Raymond Jean denies any erotic symbolism in Simon's novels, arguing that "nous sommes très loin de tout ce qui peut lier le désir à une transgression [Bataille] . . .L'amour chez lui, loin de supposer éloignement ou recul, implique le contact et la fusion des corps, met en jeu une totalité sensorielle vécue et décrite dans la 'participation,' se situe volontiers à un niveau que l'on pourrait appeler 'vitaliste' et même 'nutritionnel.' "[19] But while we might agree that the nature of physical love is on one level nutritional in Simon's fiction, the sensual union of the passive male child and the nourishing mother figure is never complete. Still, Jean's argument does not necessarily conflict with John Fletcher's remarks that "le sentiment de la culpabilité, de la honte, et la certitude d'avoir 'transgressé un interdit' (*BP*, 139), sont toujours présents à l'esprit du narrateur simonien."[20] Rather than negate one another, the respective interpretations of Jean and Fletcher reveal the paradoxical nature of physical encounters in Simon's texts. For more often than not, dependent sensual passivity is followed by flagrant erotic aggression as the narrators try desperately to escape from a discontinuous self through the timeless fusion of erotic frenzy.

Feelings of guilt are understandably absent from the narrators' descriptions of the protective mother archetype because their relationship with her centers around a framework of legitimate, soothing sensuality rather than forbidden transgression. Nevertheless, as an encounter intensifies, the narrator's sensual images of nature invariably yield to erotic images of animals and ancient mythological heroes, and with this latter imagery, guilt feelings become apparent. Hence Corinne's lack of modesty and shame in the woods appalls as well as fascinates the narrator in *Histoire:* "elle pas plus émue ni troublée que si elle n'avait fait que ça depuis sa naissance l'ogive de son ventre étroit dénudé impudique se relevant entreprenant de me l'essuyer maladroitement avec son mouchoir l'âne d'Apulée copuler moi vaguement écoeuré" (*HI*, 342). In effect, the narrator is disturbed by the young woman's refusal to feel ashamed about her conduct and especially about her nudity. His reaction indicates that he considers such bestial behavior taboo (notice the reference once again to "l'âne d'Apulée) and that by engaging in it, Corinne, herself, should also feel guilty.

Although Fletcher offers no explanations for the narrators' sense of culpability, one can be found by examining each speaker's images of his mother. In both *Histoire* and *La Bataille de Pharsale*, the narrator's mother is the direct antithesis of the voluptuous, free-spirited sexual partner. In fact, the narrator in

Histoire corrclatcs his mother's formal handwriting with a sexually-repressed personality: "l'écriture épineuse hautaine aussi rigide dans le plaisir la volupté que dans les années de virginité" (*HI*, 401). Stricken with illness at an early age, his mother is further referred to as "un de ces animaux traqués affolés et martyrisés, haletant, sur les fastueux coussins de dentelle semblables à une parure de mariée" (*HI*, 389). Time and again, the narrator pictures her as a virgin and martyr, the symbol of self-renunciation. As a result, she becomes inextricably linked to the concepts of purity, suffering, and martyrdom.

Perhaps the most revealing distinctions between mother and lover occur in *La Bataille de Pharsale* when the narrator remembers his pervading sense of misconduct as a young man in the presence of an alluring sexual partner. He then passes immediately to memories of childhood misbehavior and, with such a transition, suggests that the fear of worrying his mother over his activity was the initial basis for many of his later feelings of guilt:

> parfois au milieu de l'après-midi il m'arrivait de la trouver sortant à peine du lit encore à *demi nue tiède* trainant dans ce kimono dénoué grignotant n'importe quoi quelque chose resté de la veille me rendant compte à présent que cette *violente attraction* qu'elle exerçait sur moi avait ce même goût cette sorte d'*amer parfum de défendu* de chatoyant et de pauvre que je respirais enfant confondu avec l'écoeurante odeur d'acétylène qui flotte en permanence dans les foires et qui pour moi avait fini par s'identifier à la *notion même de culpabilité de désastre*

> m'attardant bien au-delà de *l'heure autorisée* c'est-à-dire celle qui m'aurait permis de raconter un mensonge crédible me sentant peu à peu envahi par *cette irrémédiable angoisse* faite à la fois de remords et de défi sachant qu'il était déjà horriblement tard que j'aurais dû être rentré depuis longtemps que maman s'inquiétait et que *chaque minute augmentait encore l'ampleur de la catastrophe* non pas une punition mais pouvant voir à l'avance son visage empâté gras empreint de cette *expression douloureuse* que l'on peut voir à *ces saintes des peintures baroques* avec leur double menton

> leurs mains tordues dans le bouillonnement des draperies
> leurs yeux pleins de larmes théâtralement levés vers le
> ciel et le dîner retardé. . . (*BP*, 50-51, italics mine)

The narrator's juxtaposition of the two women in this passage
is notably striking as he moves from remembrances of a violent-
ly attractive female, half-naked in her loosened kimono, to
earlier memories of his mother's pained expression, resembling
those baroque portraits of weary and tormented saints.   Ap-
parently, when the narrator misbehaved as a child, he felt that
he added to his mother's suffering, becoming more and more
responsible for it.   Uncle Charles further accentuated the young
narrator's sense of guilt with such remarks as: "tu pourrais
quelquefois penser au chagrin que tu fais à ta mère" (*BP*, 53).
The underlying irony, of course, is marked by the fact that the
imminent catastrophe referred to in the passage is little more
than "le dîner retardé."

By associating later feelings of culpability in sex to his
childhood guilt over maternal disapproval, O. demonstrates
that even after his mother's death he still felt accountable to her
for his behavior.   And in fact, the narrator in *Histoire* admits
that he was reminded of his mother's presence long after her
death:

> me dit que du haut du ciel maman me regardait
>
> l'imaginant non pas avec ce visage plein rieur un peu
> gras qu'elle avait jeune fille lorsqu'elle posait drapée
> dans un châle déguisée en Espagnole mais ce masque en
> lame de couteau émacié et martyrisé la joue décharnée
> appuyée sur un poing nonchalamment accoudée au rebord
> de la loge. . . (*HI*, 366)

Unlike the nourishing mother figure or the erotic partner, the
narrator's real mother belongs to a realm of renunciation and
suffering.   Even during her youth, she showed continued physical
restraint.   For him, she was the epitome of respectability and
decency: "elle pareille—avec son corps caché sous les rigides
baleines des corsets, les rigides et bruissantes jupes, son visage
serein enduit de décentes crèmes et de décents voiles de poudre—
à l'un de ces hauts murs nus bordant une rue, impénétrables,
hautains, secrets, dont seuls dépassent les sommets de touffes de

lauriers ou de camélias aux inviolables fleurs immobiles dans les sombres et rigides verdures" (*HI*, 20). Calm, angular, tastefully made-up, and amply clothed, she is indeed the polar opposite of the luminescent, curvaceous, and semi-clothed or nude women who populate the narrators' sexual encounters and fantasies.

Whether consciously or sub-consciously, each narrator seems aware that his erotic adventures have run contrary to his mother's moral code. But rather than prevent sexual transgression, the notion of violating a maternal taboo merely adds to the attraction of the act itself. As a result, an aura of taboo surrounds all the physically stimulating, animal-like females in Simon's novels. For as subjects of prohibition, these erotic partners are basically *sacred*.[21] The following passage gives support to this interpretation, describing the nephew in *Histoire* as he remembers himself kneeling in front of Corinne, the great whore, and likens himself to Saint Polycarp, an ancient Christian martyr: "agenouillé devant elle entre ses cuisses comme pour faire ma prière tendant vers elle ce porphyresque quel est donc aussi ce saint hagios ermite au nom grec Porphyre Polycarpe Polyphile ou quoi lui aussi agenouillé en prière au sommet d'une colonne dans le désert restant je ne sais combien de jours. . .et cette courtisane Babylone la grande prostituée" (*HI*, 343). Drunken with the wine of fornication, Georges kneels to the new Babylon, the biblical mother of harlots who allegedly perverted the inhabitants of the earth.[22] Corinne is thereby transformed into an archetypal whore who lays herself open to be desired and possessed. Bataille has further noted that, in an erotic context, "prostitution is the logical consequence of the feminine attitude. . .By the care she lavishes on her toilet, by the concern she has for her beauty set off by her adornment, a woman regards herself as an object always trying to attract men's attention. Similarly if she strips naked she reveals the object of a man's desire, an individual and particular object to be prized."[23] Momentarily driven away from woman by the terror of misconduct, Simon's narrators are therefore drawn back to her by an irrepressible attraction and adoration for "the taboo would forbid the transgression but the fascination compels it."[24]

Reflecting on their pasts, the narrators of *La Route des Flandres, Histoire,* and *La Bataille de Pharsale* also link their erotic adventures with earlier experiences of human violence and warfare since the domain of eroticism is also the domain of violence, of violation.[25]   J. Sturrock has argued on more general grounds that all human and social relationships in Simon's novels are based on aggression.[26]   Yet such a claim seems difficult to substantiate within the texts themselves. Nevertheless, it is clear that Simon's narrators frequently refer to ancient mythological heroes as well as to contemporary literary figures like Proust's Marcel and Swann, in order to mark the universality of erotic violence and suffering. Such associations indicate that the narrators accept eroticism, suffering in love, and solitude as indigenous to all societies, past and present.

It appears that in one way or another, physical suffering and violence characterize almost all of the erotic activity in the Simonian text. For like all violent encounters, the sexual act is, in one sense, merely another physiological variation on the theme of "l'introduction d'un objet non seulement dur mais capable de répandre, projeter avec violence hors de lui et comme un prolongement liquide de lui-même cette impétueuse laitance, ce jaillissement" (*RF,* 192). Experiencing both the power and savage brutality of his own sexuality, Georges quite literally battles with Corinne in order to convince her of his love and devotion, and the female protagonist of *L'Herbe* continually returns to images of her in-laws engaged in a sexual battle that frequently takes on mythic overtones. Likewise, the narrator in *La Bataille de Pharsale,* who remembers coming to the door only to realize that the woman he loves is with another man, imagines the aggressive fury of their love-making in fierce and explosive terms: "sa gorge quand il s'enfonce de nouveau en elle faisant entendre un bruit comme si elle s'étouffait articulant des mots entrecoupés puis elle se mit simplement à crier" (*BP,* 176-177). This same image appears in expanded or contracted form throughout the novel. Its recurrence accentuates the obsessive nature of the narrator's mind: "au moment précis où il pénètre dans son con sa bouche fait entendre un bruit étranglé, comme si elle souffoquait, s'étouffait" (*BP,* 213). The image continues to haunt him because he has been unsuccessful in dealing with the situation and its message: that complete physical union is only momentary and that the human heart is inconstant. Eventually all partners are betrayed.

In *Histoire,* the nephew-narrator repeatedly conjures up a childhood memory of blood trickling down Corinne's leg. The image evokes the same strange sexuality that Simon's narrators find in warfare, since injuries and suffering commonly hold an erotic appeal. For Georges, Corinne's body is also linked to the ancient sacrificial alter used for war offerings. On it, her husband, de Reixach, suffered and was crucified: "le lieu le centre l'autel n'en était pas une colline chauve, mais ce suave et tendre et vertigineux et broussailleux et secret repli de la chain. . . Ouais: crucifié, agonisant sur l'autel la bouche l'antre de. . ." (*RF*, 13). But since Georges does not perceive Corinne's cruelty as an individual or highly stylized trait, he offers no condemnation. She is merely a representative of her sex and a master guide to erotic adventure. By viewing her in this fashion, he annuls any historical or personal peculiarities. Georges would rather connect Corinne's aggressive nature to the brutal behavior of mankind's primitive ancestors: "la peau très blanche en haut de la cuisse se teintant d'un bistre clair à partir de l'aine, les lèvres de la fente d'un bistre plus prononcé avant l'endroit où commence la muqueuse comme s'il restait persistait là mal effacé quelque chose de nos ancêtres sauvages primitifs sombres s'étreignant s'accouplant roulant nus violents et brefs dans la poussière les fourrés" (*RF*, 275).

The narrative consciousness in *La Bataille de Pharsale* continually moves backward and forward in Time in an effort to repossess an image of self, but although his fragmented thoughts and memories jump from one incident to another, without any apparent logic, the structural juxtaposition of memory patterns is significant. Accordingly, flashbacks of erotic relations intersperse earlier war images, reinforcing the similarities between the two activities. For this reason, passages emphasizing the brute force in erotic behavior are common occurrences in *La Bataille de Pharsale*:

> javelots épées lances comme ce jeu de jonchets dont
> il s'agit de sortir l'une après l'autre les petites pièces
> crochues pourvues de barbes de pointes pilum frappant
> entrant et ressortant à plusieurs reprises de la blessure le
> renflement de sa pointe triangulaire arrachant aux lèvres
> le sang jaillissant par saccades brûlant Elle m'inonda se
> mit à hoqueter et crier balbutiant des mots sans suite
> donnant de violents coups de reins (*BP*, 40)

The imagistic movement of this passage is such that javelins, swords, spears, wounds, and blood all prefigure the cries and

fury of an erotic encounter. Moreover, in love as in war, the de-
mands made on the body are extreme; erotic activity produces
gasps and suffocating sensations which remind Simon's narrators
of the vital signs of approaching death in a wartime setting. In
fact, the narrator's body comes so close to an erotic death ex-
perience in *Histoire* that he imagines himself as a dead warrior
or hunter from prehistoric times:

> ma pine enfoncée en elle moi etendu rigide mort pouvant
> me voir sous la forme de ce guerrier ou chasseur ithy-
> phallique de la préhistoire réduit à quelques traits char-
> bonneux comme si j'étais fait de barres raidi tout mon
> corps aux membres durcis noirs mes os parallèles qu'on
> retrouverait des siècles plus tard dessinés sur les parois
> des cavernes ou poussière dans la poussière comme ce
> mort au casque ou à la tête d'oiseau allongé sanglant. . .
> (*HI*, 125-126)

Ultimately, death becomes the prevailing goal of love in
Simon's fiction. As Bataille describes it, "the urge towards
love, pushed to its limit is an urge toward death."[27] A simulated
sensation of death at the apex of love-making is a desirable end
because it offers each narrator a feeling of continuity and time-
lessness, as well as the sensation of union with something outside
himself. Simon draws further attention to the significance of
the death wish by prefacing Part III of *La Route des Flandres*
with a definitional framework by Malcolm de Chazal: "la
volupté, c'est l'étreinte d'un corps de mort par deux êtres vivants.
Le 'cadavre' dans ce ces, c'est le temps assassiné pour un temps
et rendu consubstantiel au toucher" (*RF,* 253). Here and else-
where, Simon stresses the progressive erosion of Time that
appears to be momentarily arrested in sexual climax and in
death. For an instant, lovers destroy their self-contained exis-
tences by moving beyond *self*-consciousness to an awareness of
self-and-other. Uprooted in this manner from their previously
enclosed worlds, Georges and Corinne enter a realm of seemingly
eternal continuity:

> morts elle et moi assourdis par le vacarme de notre sang
> se ruant refluant en grondant dans nos membres se pré-
> cipitant à travers les ramifications compliquées de nos
> artères comme comment appelle-t-on cela mascaret je
> crois toutes les rivières se mettant à couler en sens inverse

remontant vers leurs sources, comme si nous avions un
instant été vidés tout entiers comme si notre vie tout
entière s'était précipitée avec un bruit de cataracte vers
et hors de nos ventres s'arrachant s'extirpant de nous de
moi de ma solitude se libérant s'élançant au dehors se
répandant jaillissant sans fin. . . (*RF*, 265-265)

As described in the passage above, the rush of blood and
the ejaculation that constitutes a sexual climax upset the normal
physiological balance of the organism to such an extent that it is
violently loosened from its common habitat. With the emission
of sexual fluid, it is as if the two human bodies and spirits follow
the same route outward, emptying into the other, and thereby
destroying all previously established boundaries. In principle,
then, the sexual urge and climax signal the potential destruction
of barriers in death-like oblivion for "just as the violence of
death overturns—irrevocably—the structure of life so temporarily
and partially does sexual violence."[28]

The Enigmatic Female

However, like most of Simon's narrators, Georges discovers
that, in the final analysis, erotic union is not infinite. In love's
aftermath, the walls separating him from Corinne reappear.
Once again, they are the unhappy prisoners of their own bodies:
"mais ce n'était pas vrai: un instant seulement en réalité. . .
quelque chose de furieux frustré hurlant alors dans notre solitude
frustrée, de nouveau emprisonné, heurtant avec fureur les parois
les étroites et indépassables limites" (*RF*, 265). The empty
"armoire" in their hotel room becomes a symbol for all the
empty, rented rooms of lovers who fail to fulfill their erotic
aspirations. Cognizant of an identical need to escape from the
confines of self, the narrator in *Histoire* also admits to failure:
"je ne pouvais voir que ses cheveux blonds son dos comme un
mur énigmatique enfermant cachant cette espèce de tragique
mélancolie" (*HI*, 109-110). Like separate houses, each member
of the couple is an entity unto himself, walled off from his re-
spective partner with only windows from which to gaze out on
the other.

In their solitude, both Georges and the nephew in *Histoire* experience fusion with woman as a fleeting instance rather than an eternal union. Bataille accounts for this inevitable disappointment after climax by explaining that the goal of love is the "total blending of two beings, a continuity between two discontinuous creatures. Hence love spells suffering for us in so far as it is a quest for the impossible."[29] A lasting union would deny the discontinuous nature of man's being in a fragmentary universe. Unable to transcend this discontinuity, however, Simon's narrators suffer from their individual separateness. Despite all attempts, woman remains an alien being and a symbol for the unfathomable mysteries of the life process. Even in her role as guide to the unknown, she retains the essence of those mysteries that define her sex: "quelque chose de mystérieux délicat et un peu terrifiant dont je savais que je serais à jamais exclu maladies qu'elles seules pouvaient avoir dans leurs mystérieux et délicats organes et dont quoi qu'il fasse mon corps à moi ne pourrait même pas imaginer l'existence" (*HI,* 309).

Odette and Albertine

Suggesting a similar personal discovery, the narrator in *La Bataille de Pharsale* recites a line from Proust over and over in his mind: "petite cellule particulière qu'est un être" (*BP,* 85). Like Proust's principle characters, he cannot successfully merge with another because he too is unable to shed his self-contained existence.[30] And as the recurring leit-motif "je souffrais comme" indicates, the theme of suffering dominates a major portion of *La Bataille de Pharsale.* Having rejected physical love as a means of lasting union and movement out of self, the narrator is left with only the memory of his torment and frustration. Transformed by suffering, earlier images of Hélène have been irrevocably tarnished by his subsequent pain.

The theme of suffering gains additional prominence with the narrator's incorporation of fragmentary quotations from *A la recherche du temps perdu.* Functioning much the same way as the earlier quote from Apuleius, the two passages that follow produce multiple mirrored reflections as Simon's narrator identi-

fies himself with Proust's Marcel, who in turn, identifies himself
with Swann:

> 'ce nouveau sourire qu'elle lui avait adressé le
> soir même et qui inverse maintenant raillait
> Swann et se chargeait d'amour pour un autre de
> cette inclinaison de sa tête mais renversée sous
> d'autres lèvres' (*BP*, 168)

> 'combinée avec ces images la souffrance en avait fait
> aussitôt quelque chose d'absolument différent de ce que
> peut être pour toute autre personne une dame en gris un
> pourboire une douche toutes ces images ma souffrance les
> avait immédiatement altérées en leur matière même je ne
> les voyais pas dans la lumière qui éclaire le spectacle de la
> terre c'était le fragment d'un autre monde d'une planète
> inconnue et maudite une vue de' (*BP*, 169)

For Swann, Marcel, and Simon's narrators, suffering caused by
suspicion and distance alters their memories of the women they
loved. Whether willfully done or not, Odette and Albertine
abuse Proust's protagonists much the way Corinne and Hélène
do in Simon's texts by inspiring an image of constancy and union
that they can never live out on a day to day basis. In yet another
passage lifted from *A la recherche*, Simon's narrator reproduces
Proust's sound patterns rather than the quotation's actual spell-
ing, but the subject matter remains the same: the infidelity of
love. It causes both Swann and Marcel to regret their passion,
knowing how quickly it will be betrayed (*BP*, 178-179).

The narrator's disappointment in *Histoire* parallels Georges'
earlier remarks in *La Route des Flandres*. After love-making, his
sense of unity and continuity dissolves in a similar fashion.
Once again, he acknowledges woman as other, as an object out-
side himself, and love's promise of infinite union as a sham: "puis
se rendant compte tout à coup que pour la première fois il
l'entendait respirer prenant pour la première fois conscience de
cette chose (mais comment dire: existence, vie, autre?) ex-
térieure à lui maintenant étendue gisant à côté de lui dans le
noir à la fois plate presque inexistante et pourtant haute comme
une montagne. . ." (*HI*, 374-375). Seen in this light, erotic fusion
is never more than a chemical reaction, having a marked be-
ginning and an all too abrupt end. Thus, as in *A la recherche*, the

realities of love fail to meet each narrator's personal ideal. And in each case, the realization of another's deception causes great individual suffering.

Deianeira

The narrator in *Histoire* laments not only the loss of his mother's love, resulting from a lengthy illness and premature death, but also the memory of Hélène and the subsequent loss of love between them. Although they have separated, Hélène's image and the suffering she has caused him permeate the novel from beginning to end. However idyllic their union appeared at its inception, the narrator soon recognized their unalterable separateness. In the following paragraphs, his mind flashes back to scenes from an earlier trip to Greece:

> malheureux tous les deux non de cette dispute absurde à l'hôtel mais de cette impossibilité emmurés désespérés chacun devant une vitrine différente à chacune des extrémités de la salle moi l'épiant à la dérobée elle regardant ou faisant semblant d'être absorbée par la contemplation des débris. . .

> prêts à tomber (les mots), aurait-on dit, en une poussière de particules friables brunâtres de rouille qui semblait s'échapper des pages du dictionnaire en même temps qu'un impalpable et subtil relent de cendres, comme le résidu, les indestructibles décombres de ces villes anéanties par quelque séisme, l'éruption d'un volcan, la pluie de feu, et où les cadavres des couples enlacés subsistent intacts, momifiés, ardents, insoucieux, juvéniles et priapiques dans un désordre de trépieds, de coupes renversées. . . (*HI*, 109-110)

What we find, here, is a marked disparity between real and ideal love as the narrator recalls his inability to penetrate the secret walls dividing himself from Hélène. The juxtaposition of mobile and immobile lovers lays further stress on the lack of permanent fusion among the living. In this fashion, he contrasts the slow death of their love with the ideal union of ancient lovers found in the ashes of Pompeii and Herculaneum.

Affirming the mythic dimension of love's deception, the narrator aligns his own suffering in love with the tortures Hercules endured during his many labours. The piercing sound of a bird outside his window triggers the following mythological assocation:

> chaque fois qu'il lançait son cri avec cette sorte d'obstina-tion d'acharnement monotone absurde déchirant le tym-pan, cherchant le nom de ce lac repère d'oiseaux aux serres d'airain au bec d'airain aux plumes d'airain mangeurs de chair humaine Tympanon instrument de musique Stymphale noirs sans doute de plumage. . . (*HI*, 38)

The narrator has thus linked the bird's screeching sounds to those presumably made by the Stymphalian birds, who, accord-ing to Greek myths, ate humans with their tremendous iron beaks and destroyed crops with their droppings. For one of his many arduous labours, Hercules was commanded to drive the birds away. The nephew in *Histoire* has therefore likened his suffering in love to the torturous image of giant birds attack-ing the ancient hero.

It would be relatively easy to overlook the significance of the mythological reference to Hercules and the Stymphalian birds if there were no further elaborations in the text, but the narrator also refers later to Hélène as Deianeira, the wife of Hercules. In a similar fashion, Louise associates the brutality of her in-laws' love-making and the apparent loneliness of their life together with images of an aging Hercules and Deianeira (*HE*, 226-227). Ancient myths recount how the centaur, Nessus, attempted to violate Deianeira while carrying her across a river. Enraged, Hercules struck the Centaur with an arrow. But before Nessus died, he gave his blood to Deianeira, instructing her to use it as a love charm on Hercules in order to speed his return home. Fearing her husband's infidelity, she covered his tunic with the centaur's blood to woo him back to her. Nessus, how-ever, had tricked Deianeira. The blood became poison and cor-roded Hercules' flesh. He tore off the tunic, but his flesh was ripped away with it. He then ascended a pyre that was struck by lightening and instantly consumed, but the gods received him and he became immortal.

Simon's narrator in *Histoire* connects his suffering over the loss of love to that of Hercules after Deianeira's innocent betrayal. Hélène's image tortures him to such an extent that, like Hercules' poisoned tunic, he would tear it off, if he could: "je voudrais je voudrais je voudrais si je pouvais l'enlever l'arracher de moi retrouver la fraîcheur l'oubli Déjanire" (*HI*, 365). Later, toward the end of the novel, the images of the Stymphalian birds and of Hercules' gnawing tunic merge in the narrator's mind. Remembering Hélène's tearfilled eyes, the narrator experiences the intensity of both mythological events as her image both burns and tears at his flesh simultaneously:

> larmes dans ses yeux J'ai dit Mais tu le sais tu le sais tu le sais emplissant les coupes de ses yeux brillant suspendues au bord des cils mais sans déborder bombées tremblotant capillarité ou quoi impossible de trouver le mot cristal liquide tandis qu'ils s'élargissaient peu à peu s'agrandissaient sombres dévoraient son visage comme des taches sur un buvard si je pouvais l'arracher de moi brûlante me consumant me
>
> me déchirant dans le noir becs acérés chuchotements au-dessous du silence dans l'odeur de plâtre effrité de tristesse de mort. . . (*HI*, 381-382)

Thus, all three narrators consistently fail to sustain the timeless ecstasy found in the physical union of male and female. And as in *A la recherche,* it is love's inconstancy that causes still further grief: "les deux formes blafardes confuses sur ce lit où elle et moi aimés tout ce que j'aurais voulu c'était cela ne jamais en connaître une autre ne jamais Je voudrais quitte-la Ne la revois plus" (*HI,* 369). But the pain endured enables them to accept the only real future of the human body, that of frailty, death, and decomposition.

Whether hidden or nude, possessed or viewed from afar, the female figure lures Simon's narrators with the secrets of her body and the mysteries of the life process. While gazing at the photo of a nude woman, however, the nephew in *Histoire* realizes that nudity itself does not expose all of the complexities of the feminine form. Certainly, her secrets cannot be reduced to any logical formula:

> immobilisée dans cette pose paisible, banale, sa paisible
> et banale nudité tellement dépourvue de mystère qu'il
> en émanait cette espèce de mystère au second degré caché
> au-delà du visible, du palpable, cette terrifiante énigme,
> insoluble, vertigineuse, comme celle que pose le rocher,
> le nuage, l'esprit décontenancé disant: ':Qui? Simple-
> ment du silex, de la chaux, des gouttelettes d'eau?—Mais
> quoi encore? Rien que de la peau, des cheveux, des
> muqueuses? Mais quoi encore? Quoi encore? Encore?
> Encore? Encore?" (*HI*, 283)

Indeed, each quest for coalescence with the enigmatic female seems as perennial as myth itself and explains why she is repeatedly described in universal terms: memories of Corinne, Hélène, or the farm woman merge with mythological and archetypal images of Albertine, Odette, Leda, Lucius' matron, Pasiphae, and the Good Mother. Through women, the narrators seek the comforting pleasures of sensual nourishment and erotic union, but invariably fail in their flight from solitude: "tout seul sous la pluie grise, parmi les rails, les wagons de charbon, ou peut-être des années plus tard, toujours seul (quoi qu'il fût maintenant couché à côté d'une tiède chair de femme)" (*RF*, 187).

Ultimately, mythological and archetypal imagery express each narrator's conscious or unconscious yearning for a renewed stability in a disordered universe because they disclose man's "need to comprehend his own history and to discover some meaning and order in its record of violence and failure."[31] In love as in war, only fragmentary images of archetypal situations emerge from the universal flux, but they are all that man can salvage from the otherwise overwhelming chaos of his personal past.

NOTES

[1]Mircea Eliade, *Images and Symbols,* trans. by Philip Mairet (1952; rpt. New York: Sheed and Ward, 1969), p. 14 (italics mine).

[2]Claud DuVerlie has recently noted that "all in all Simon's very particular brand of eroticism aims at retaining from the beginning the most universal function of eroticism, which is to be an instrument for knowing the world, a way of apprehending reality." See Claud DuVerlie, "*Amor Interruptus:* The Question of Eroticism or, Eroticism in Question in the Works of Claude Simon," in *Sub-Stance,* 8 (Winter, 1974), pp. 21-33.

[3]Ludovic Janvier, *Une Parole exigeante* (Paris: Minuit, 1964), p. 93.

[4]Norman O. Brown, *Life Against Death* (Middleton, Connecticut: Wesleyan University Press, 1959), p. 41.

[5]*Ibid.,* p. 40.

[6]Erich Neumann, *The Origins and History of Consciousness,* trans. by R. F. C. Hull (1949; rpt. Princeton: Princeton University Press, 1971), p. 40.

[7]Eliade, *Images and Symbols,* p. 15.

[8]I shall rely on Georges Bataille's general definition of eroticism as sexual activity based on "a psychological quest independent of the natural goal: reproduction and the desire for children." Furthermore, it involves an "assenting to life even in death." See Georges Bataille, *Death and Sensuality* (New York: Walker, 1962), p. 11.

[9]*Ibid.,* p. 143.

[10]Juan Eduardo Cirlot, *A Dictionary of Symbols,* trans. by Jack Sage (New York: Philosophical Lib., 1962), p. 239.

[11]Joseph Campbell, *The Masks of God: Creative Mythology* (New York: Viking, 1971), p. 671.

[12]Sigmund Freud, *New Introductory Lectures on Psychoanalysis*, trans. by W. J. H. Sprott (London: Hogarth Press, 1933), p. 98, referred to by Norman O. Brown in *Life Against Death*, p. 175.

[13]Georges Gusdorf, *Mythe et métaphysique* (Paris: Flammarion, 1953), p. 222.

[14]Lucius Apuleius, *The Golden Ass*, trans. by William Adlington, ed. by Harry C. Schnur (New York: Crowell-Collier, 1962).

[15]In a recent article, John Fletcher cites this same passage as a description of the voluptuous Pasiphae and her bull lover. But more important, the quotation also relates the encounter of Lucius and his enamored matron. Harry Schnur translates from Chapter 46 of the Latin text as follows:

> But nothing grieved me so much as to think how I should with my huge and great legs embrace so fair a matron, or how I should touch her fine, dainty, and silken skin made of milk and honey with my hard hoofs, or how it was possible to kiss her soft, her pretty and ruddy lips with my monstrous great mouth and stony teeth, or how she, who was so young and tender, could receive my love. And I verily thought if I should hurt the woman by any kind of means, I should be thrown out to the wild beasts: but in the mean season she spoke gently to me, kissing me oft, and looked on me with burning eyes, saying: "I hold thee my cony, I hold thee my nops, my sparrow," and therewithal she shewed me that all my fear was vain, for she ofttimes embraced my body round about, and had her pleasure with me, whereby I thought the mother of Minotaurus did not causeless quence her inordinate desire with a bull. (pp. 249-250)

See John Fletcher, "Erotisme et création, ou la mort en sursis," in *Entretiens: Claude Simon*, ed. by Marcel Séguier (Toulouse: Subervie, 1972), p. 133.

[16]Apuleuis, p. 249.

[17]Gusdorf, p. 24.

[18]Bataille, p. 107.

[19]Raymond Jean, "Les Signes de l'Eros," in *Entretiens: Claude Simon*, p. 121.

[20]Fletcher, p. 138.

[21]Bataille, pp. 67-68.

[22]*The Oxford Annotated Bible: The Holy Bible*, Revised Standard Version, ed. by Herbert G. May and Bruce M. Metzger (New York: Oxford University Press, 1962), Revelations XVII, 2, 5.

[23]Bataille, p. 131.

[24]*Ibid.*, p. 68.

[25]Fletcher, p. 137.

[26]John Sturrock, *The French New Novel* (London: Oxford University Press, 1969), p. 80.

[27]Bataille, p. 42.

[28]*Ibid.*, p. 106.

[29]*Ibid.*, p. 20.

[30]Consult Françoise Van Rossum-Guyon's "De Claude Simon à Proust" for a number of textual and thematic parallels, in *Les Lettres Nouvelles* (September 1972), pp. 107-133.

[31]Lillian Feder, *Ancient Myth in Modern Poetry* (Princeton: Princeton University Press, 1971), p. 416.

III

SYMBOLIC SPATIAL JOURNEYS

Perception, says Merleau-Ponty, "is the background from which all acts stand out, and is presupposed by them."[1] From a phenomenological viewpoint, the world is always perceived by *some*one at *some* moment in Time and as such, can never be grasped in its entirety. Yet the limited perspective of an individual consciousness, a narrative technique so predominant in the *nouveau roman*, should not be invalidated on a general basis merely because of its inherent subjectivity. On the contrary, it seems that each self-reflecting consciousness in Simon's fiction comprehends in large part the essential properties at work in the cosmos and expresses this understanding through his use of archetypal imagery.

Each narrator knows himself only insofar as he comes to recognize the fundamental nature of the role he plays as a being in Time and in the world. In the preceding sections, we have examined the archetypal and mythological symbols associated with love and war because of the overriding import given these transpersonal activities in Simon's fiction. For his narrators, however, the theatre of initiation in preparation for self-knowledge may also take place within the confines of the modern technological city or in Nature,[2] settings which likewise form an integral part of their everyday existence in the world. We find that, whether in Nature or in the city, initiation means estrangement since the laws governing these two domains deprive man of his ontological security. For both the natural world and the metropolis engender chaotic, dehumanizing, the destructive forces which, when unleashed, threaten to demolish any and all continuity of self. The narrator's response to the alienation that menaces the self in Nature and in the city is two-fold: either submission or escape. When liberation is sought, they attempt to extract themselves from the subterranean caverns and labyrinths which comprise the contemporary city by lifting their eyes and thoughts toward the boundless Heavens or, when exposed to hazards of Nature, they retreat into the house or shelter that most intimately protects them from the world outside.

The following section will delineate the nightmarish qualities of the city and the dangers of the natural world as they are contrasted with the protective aura of the Heavens and the enclosed shelter. Through a process of phenomenological reductionism, the city and Nature, coupled with the Heavens and the personal shelter, all reveal the distinctly archetypal images of space which lie behind each narrator's subjective perspective. Thus conceived, the quantified physical space of our technological age yields to the qualitative space of myth in Simon's novels, for both the designated space and the narrator's reactions to it have a transtemporal significance.[3] The dynamic tension that exists between inner and outer, upward and downward, is such that descent into the city is most often contrasted with a desire for flight toward the Heavens, while the threatening immensity of Mother Earth is similarly countered with a need for the secure environment of a house or like structure. These contradictory spatial experiences are repeatedly juxtaposed for shock value, much the way Eisenstein himself had contrasted cinemagraphic images for montage purposes.[4] The reader or film viewer must make sense out of the immediate conflict of images rather than attempt to decipher the logic of their linear sequence.

By opposing contradictory spatial sensations in this fashion, the narrators transform a seemingly chaotic cosmos into a universe of modern myths and symbols since their relationships to various spatial regions reveal crucial images from their own unconscious which unquestionably mark the survival of archaic symbolisms in the psyche of modern man. The successful initiate is he who recognizes the archetypal quality of these relationships and, in so doing, reintegrates his *self* with the psychological, historical, and cosmic rhythms. Experienced in this way, the world "is no longer an opaque mass of objects arbitrarily thrown together," but instead, as Eliade concludes, "a living cosmos, articulated and meaningful. In the last analysis, 'the world reveals itself as language.' It speaks to man through its own mode of being, through its structures and its rhythms."[5]

The City as Underworld

According to many myths and mystery religions, the aspiring initiate must endure the dangers met in the spatial construct of a labyrinth or underworld in order to complete his initiatory ordeal. Entering the underworld, labyrinth, mouth of a monster, or innumerable other variants of this rite, signifies a descent into the cosmic night or the horror and chaos of Hell. Furthermore, emergence from this frightful experience invariably brings about the creation of a new world or, at the very least, a new mode of being. In effect, "the mystery of initiation discloses to the neophyte, little by little, the true dimensions of existence; by introducing him to the sacred, the mystery obliges him to assume the responsibilities of a man."[6]

From a psychological viewpoint, descent into the underworld or labyrinth actually describes a temporal and existential fall into fear and nightmare: "la descente risque à tout instant de se confondre et de se transformer en chute."[7] A number of psychologists and philosophers have speculated that this fear of falling begins in man's earliest moments of consciousness with his first attempts at upright movement: "pour le bipède vertical que nous sommes, le sens de la chute et de la pesanteur accompagne toutes nos premières tentatives autocinétiques et locomotrices. . .il se pourrait qu'elle [la chute] soit l'expérience douloureuse fondamentale et constitue pour la conscience la composante dynamique de toute représentation du mouvement et de la temporalité."[8] Hence man's notion of the fall is not derived merely from an imagined time but, as Gilbert Durand and Gaston Bachelard have both noted, from an existentially lived time: "nous imaginons l'élan vers le haut et nous connaissons la chute vers le bas."[9] The inevitability of the fall reminds man of his own terrestrial limitations, of his mortality, and of his inescapable humanness.

For the modern city dweller in Simon's fiction, the *métro*, that is to say the *sub*way or *under*ground, is by far the most closely analogous symbol for the archetypal underworld of ancient myths or mystery religions. The image of the métro first suggests to the narrator in *La Bataille de Pharsale* the incredibly mundane, mechanical, and repetitive aspects of our current technological societies where "les gens continuent toujours à sortir du métro à intervalles à peu près réguliers toujours par fournées correspondant aux arrivées des rames" (*BP*, 96). However, more important associations remind him of those renowned infernos of the ancients, as in *The Aeneid*, for example, where Aeneas endures the perils and tortures of the underworld: "enfers aux voûtes de porcelaine blanche émaillée parfumés à la créosote. Dans *l'Enéide* ou quoi?. . .les récifs noirs aux noms de monstres cernées d'écume" (*BP*, 17). Bernard, the young protagonist of Simon's *Le Sacre du printemps* (1954), has a remarkably similar vision of the underground métro with its smell of ammonia and human sweat, "l'odeur même du travail, de la colère et de la malédiction stagnant sous les voûtes aux parois vernissées. . ." (*SP*, 92). For O., the enigmatic narrator in *La Bataille de Pharsale,* the métro's fiery beauty and harsh sterility have created a modern psychological as well as physical counterpart to the blazing underworlds of antiquity.

The train station in *Histoire,* as well as in *Le Palace,* forms part of a sub-terrestrial network connecting cavernous cities inhabited by cyclopean machines: "la voix du haut-parleur inhumaine la voix de Cyclope métallique égrenant les noms des villes caverneuse formidable BARCELONE-EXPRESS" (*HI,* 366). The excessive heat and lack of fresh air in the subway or train station, coupled with such mechanical means of communication as dehumanized loud speakers and the apparently uniform indifference of the masses, constitute the modern underground Hell. Scratched onto tombstones or sprayed on the subway walls, the irreverent, oftentimes unintelligible graffitti of our times have become the predominant language of his new technological complex: "une frénétique accumulation de signes dépourvus de sens, les bizarres et laborieux bégaiements d'un idiot, les incompréhensibles vestiges d'un langage incohérent" (*HI,* 378). Of course, the underlying irony in images such as these stems from the inference that civilized man no longer has need of gods or primordial ancestors to construct or dictate his trials and tortures in a mythological underworld. Modern civilization, when left to its own devices, creates similar worlds all by itself.

The narrator in *La Bataille de Pharsale* also evokes the mythological image of the labyrinth and aligns it with an allusion to the Catholic concept of Purgatory when describing the métro and the adjacent underground lavatories. His images emphasize the complexity of movement below the surface as well as the notion of sin and salvation because those who emerge from the city's putrid depths may, in fact, be saved: "dans l'odeur ammoniacale d'urine et de désinfectant le silence souterrain ponctué à intervalles réguliers par les bruits des chasses d'eau à déclenchement automatique tous à la queue leu leu errant dans les corridors compliqués de ce comment appelle-t-on l'endroit où vont les petits enfants morts avant d'avoir été baptisés?" (*BP*, 15-16). We are reminded here of Zola's stifling underworld vision in *Germinal*, where miners descend daily into a veritable hell of gas, dust, and ink-like darkness.

The same narrator of *La Bataille de Pharsale* further expands on the image of descent and entrapment below the surface of the city by describing the entrance to the jupiterian métro as a large mouth before which Jesus is seated. Later, he refers back to this image in a curious passage that combines both Greek and Catholic mythology in the revered figures of Achilles, Jesus, and the Holy Ghost, who sit waiting to redeem those who come forth from the deepest places of the earth: "alors drôle d'effet s'Il trônait là sur le trottoir appuyé sur sa croix comme Achille sur sa lance entouré de nuages d'ouate hydrophile en face de la bouche du métro le Saint Esprit suspendu au-dessus de sa tête" (*BP*, 169). Seen in this manner, the métro is our modern monster, swallowing initiates in large numbers with mechanically indifferent precision. Salvation occurs only after both a mental and physical ascent from the métro's cavernous entrails, which are also the entrails of the contemporary city itself.

Like the voyage to the underworld or into the labyrinth, descent into the mouth of the métro thereby represents a symbolic death and rebirth, provided, of course, that the neophyte comes to terms with the significance of his initiatory experience. Reminiscent of Jonah's adventure in the belly of a whale, this descent becomes yet another variant on the initiatory ordeal of being swallowed by a monster for, as Eliade points out, "there can be no doubt that the fish that swallows Jonah and the other mythical heroes symbolises death; its belly represents Hell. In medieval visions, Hell is frequently imagined in the form of an

enormous marine monster, which perhaps had its prototype in
the biblical Leviathan. To be swallowed by it is therefore equiva-
lent to dying, to the descent into Hell."[10]

For Northrop Frye, the demonic imagery of Hell consists
of cities of destruction, dead machines, weapons of war, serpents,
labyrinths, and monsters. In direct contrast to multiple images
of Heaven, asserts Frye, "we have in this world the labyrinth
or maze, the image of lost direction, often with a monster at
its heart like the Minotaur."[11] Without wishing to accept Frye's
extreme view that all literature reflects either a displaced or un-
displaced myth, we can nevertheless agree that demonic imagery
in Simon's fiction does transform machines into objects, with
human or animal characteristics, in order to enhance still further
the nightmarish qualities of the contemporary city. Thus, the
narrator in *Histoire* remembers a car in the streets of Barcelona as
the *living* symbol for the fears and cruel passions of a city en-
meshed in the political turmoil of civil war. Immobilized be-
tween two antagonistic political groups like a surrounded beast
of prey, the car is at the mercy of its predators:

> la voiture toujours de travers immobilisée. . .l'air
> d'un animal féroce stupide pourvu de petits yeux et d'un
> cerveau plus petit encore atrophié enfermé dans une
> carapace une espèce de crustacé déposé sur le sec par une
> vague ou plutôt rhinocéros le ventre souillé de poussière
> ocre. . .arrêté immobile entre deux charges aveugles
> décontenancé marqué comme une bête de troupeau
> d'initiales d'un sigle barbouillé à la diable en grandes
> lettres blanches. . . (*HI,* 177)

Each political faction must leave a written mark on the mechan-
ical beast as a sign of organized defiance and power. Just as the
car in this passage becomes the modern symbol for captured
game or treasures, so too the people who gather around it are
associated with two ancient disputing tribes: "on aurait dit
deux tribus voisines sur un terrain de chasse contesté en train de
se disputer le dépéçage d'une grosse bête abattue palabrant sans
se comprendre dans leurs idiomes gutturaux violents" (*HI,* 188).
The implication underlying the image of the captured car has
ironic overtones because it suggests that most human disputes
begin on a small parcel of land over the possession of some rela-
tively insignificant object. So we might say that on a broader

level the car represents society's archetypal victim, symbolizing not only the subjugated prey and contested treasures or institutions of civil war Spain but also those of disputing nations, cities, or tribes both past and present.

Like the métro, the archetypal factory contributes to the infernal quality of modern civilization. For the traveling narrator in *La Bataille de Pharsale*, the factory appears to rise abruptly up out of the womb of the goddess earth only to spew forth its burning, noxious gases, as if it too were ascending from the fiery entrails of the earth. The contrast, here, between the nurturing nature figure of Diana of Epheseus, the many-breasted goddess in Roman mythology, and the deadening presence of the factory is considerable:

> comme si elle [l'usine] avait surgi entourée de son asphyxiant nuage de vapeurs brûlante et minérale des épaisseurs profondes de la terre dans un sourd fracas de choses concassées calcinées lentement écrasées par le poids de millions et de millions d'années forêts englouties pétrifiées fougères de pierre animaux poissons aux arêtes de basalte obscure gestation dans le ventre de comment s'appelait cette monumentale déesse aux multiples mamelles d'argile et de rochers. . . (*BP*, 161-162)

However, the supreme edifice and surely the most representative symbol of the modern city is the bank, an image that prevails throughout *Histoire* and even inspires the title of *Le Palace*. Replacing the great towering churches of the past, the bank has literally become the central organ around which the whole of modern society pivots: "la banque, l'espèce de temple avec ses froides colonnes de marbre veinées de gris, ses grilles de fer forgé et ses plantes vulcanisées" (*HI*, 72). Once inside the bank, the underworld is transformed into a veritable labyrinth of shiny, inorganic objects made of vinyl, rubber, and polished chrome. Within the confines of its walls, typewriter sounds, emanating from secretarial offices off the central corridor, grow to a feverish crescendo similar to that of masticating animals: "inquiétants murmures qui parviennent des profondeurs des grottes, des cavernes, mystérieux, glacés, . . .dans un froissement continu, insidieux et obsédant de mastication" (*HI*, 70-71). The secretaries themselves are viewed as the de-humanized guardians of a unique power dependent solely upon the continaul movement and exchange of man-made paper.

Even in prehistoric times, the cavern or labyrinth had a religious or spiritual significance as an initiatory arena, a symbolic way through death and rebirth.[12]   In his impressive study on *The Great Mother,* Erich Neumann concludes that "this labyrinthine way, which leads to the center of danger, where at the midnight hour, in the land of the dead, in the middle of the night sea voyage, the decision falls, occurs in the judgment of the dead in Egypt, in the mysteries both classical and primitive, and in the corresponding processes of psychic development in modern man."[13]   Likewise, the bank in *Histoire* brings into play the familiar initiatory themes of confusion, danger, and death that run throughout archaic myths and rituals.   Thus the journey through the monstrous concrete labyrinth of the modern bank, along with the struggle to combat the archetypal difficulties encountered therein, depicts the narrator's symbolic quest for freedom and life.   As the narrator himself realizes, exploring its corridors is indeed equivalent to entering the belly of a monster: "tout à fait à l'intérieur à présent (dans les entrailles pour ainsi dire) des couloirs de marbre" (*HI*, 73).   But the contemporary Jonah also resembles an updated Theseus as he fights a new breed of Minotaur which, like the bank itself, continually devours paper, checks, and memoranda at man's expense: "si Thésée faisait irruption ce serait sous l'aspect d'un gringalet gominé et armé d'une mitraillette, et qu'il l'abandonnerait non pas sur une plage mais au bord d'une route, ou à la rigueur dans une chambre d'hôtel meublé, après l'avoir soulagée de sa dot constituée de titres de puits de pétrole et de mines d'étain" (*HI*, 71).   What we discover, in effect, is that the modern-day political revolutionary who opposes the capitalistic power and wealth of the labyrinthine bank now seems to perform the exemplary heroic task.

Once inside the banker's office, Theseus undergoes another telling transformation when the narrator imagines himself as an apprehensive Oedipus in front of the questioning Sphinx: "chuchotement confidentiel confessional où le solliciteur entretient un sphinx en complet-veston de ses faiblesses maladie honteuse et malodorants besoins nommés naturels d'argent, l'oracle méditant son verdict" (*HI*, 89).   Later, the narrator cynically recasts the Sphinx' ancient riddle into the shape of a modern technological enigma: "peut-être va-t-il [le Sphinx] demander non pas quel est l'animal qui marche le matin sur quatre pattes, à midi sur deux et le soir sur trois, mais quel est celui qui ne peut ni se véhiculer, ni manger, ni se couvrir, ni s'abriter s'il ne peut pas donner de l'argent en échange, ou si vous préférez quel est cet animal qui ne peut se servir d'aucun de ses cinq sens s'il n'en possède pas un sixième sous forme de carnet de chèques" (*HI,* 99). Like the famed winged monster in *Oedipus Rex,* this modern Sphinx symbolizes what Neumann terms "the age-old foe, the dragon of the abyss,"[14] that is to say, a vengeful creature who threatens to unleash her fury upon all those who fail to respond to her self-serving questions.

The analogy established between a modern banker and a malign minotaur or Sphinx-like monster appears curiously appropriate, given the banker's ignorance of, or indifference to the commonly shared experiences of love, war, suffering, and mortality, events which constitute the eternal human dilemma in Simon's fictional world. The narrator in *Histoire* expresses his tremendous psychological distance from this contemporary monster by continually jumping back and forth from war memories or childhood recollections to cold descriptions of the banker's inexpressive face and business-like manner. Even after leaving the cavernous depths of the bank building, the narrator is haunted by his appalling encounter with the Minotaur-Sphinx, imagining him in his office-den, "tapi sur son nauséabond monceau de billets, de pièces et d'os de chevaux rongés, avec ses lunettes d'or, ses yeux froids, ses mains méticuleuses" (*HI,* 103). What jars us in this passage is the narrator's almost incidental inclusion of the image of corroding horses in wartime, a highly emotional image, which clashes so dramatically with his lucidly detailed description of the bank monster whose only concerns revolve around the perpetual acquisition and exchange of currency.

Having decided to sell much of the family furniture after the death of his uncle, the same narrator in *Histoire* is horrified by a woman-buyer who comes to make him an offer. Here, the malevolent monster waiting to prey on the narrator in the labyrinthine bank has transformed itself into a venomous spider whose crafty entrance into the family household constitutes nothing short of blasphemy. "La mangeuse de meubles," as she is called, comes to devour indifferently all that is in sight: "tapi dans un coin: énorme comme une de ces araignées dévoreuses dans ce sombre costume de veuve qu'elle s'était composé finissant de digérer ventre et sac distendus à craquer repue les yeux enfin mi-clos essuyant sur ses lèvres d'une langue grumeleuse noire les dernières traces couleur safran de poudre de bois" (*HI,* 230). The woman's sympathetic black mourning dress is merely a hypocritical ploy, masking her real intentions to consume everything of value at little expense.

Because of its hazardous character, the spider web is a common symbol of entrapment in myth or religious symbolism. According to Otto Rank's classical psychoanalytic interpretation, the female spider symbolizes the harsh mother who imprisons her own children in the meshes of her web.[15] But more than a cruel mother figure, the black Spider-Woman in this Simonian text embodies all that is deceitfully cunning, even demoniacal, in the feminine and mercantile worlds:

> elle ressemblait à un de ces insectes bardés de surfaces de carapaces polies. . .dans des besognes secrètes impérieuses ou plutôt rituelles c'est-à-dire dont les phases successives (camouflage, ruse, construction de pièges, attaques) sont commandées par les réflexes millénaires de l'espèce: quelque chose qui existerait et aurait survécu depuis les temps immémoriaux. . . (*HI,* 232)

Like the black widow spider that copulates with a male partner, then kills and eats him, the Spider-Woman is the prototype of a hardy race that has managed to survive and dominate other species since the very beginnings of combat on earth through the use of camouflage and trickery. Hence, commercial existence in the city seems no less demonic above the earth's surface than below it, despite the façade of humanitarianism that one so often encounters in the business world.

Initiation to the archetypal city means, as we have noted, descent into the cavern or labyrinth of the world below where vicious monsters lie waiting for unsuspecting victims. However, unlike the ancient Greek seamen in Homer's epics, young men of courage in Simon's modern city no longer brave underworld monsters or fabulous sea creatures. Instead, the concrete and asphalt jungles of today's city have become the modern mythological setting, a new arena which beckons them to fight the bourgeois mode of living based on "un bonheur garanti imputréscible, grâce à la production en grande série de frigidaires, d'automobiles et de postes radio" (*RF,* 188). Initiation into the Simonian metropolis introduces the narrator-neophyte to the infernal sphere of commercial existence where entire cities and nations engage in monetary battles, reflecting the fate of all things as they slowly self-destruct like disease ridden bodies: "sous la calotte de ciel déjà décoloré, blanc, la ville semble pareille à une de ces choses déssechés, mortes, ces couronnes de mariées queles vieilles femmes conservent à l'abri de globes de verre, se décomposant lentement dans l'odeur de renfermé sure, cadavérique des chambres closes" (*HI,* 365). The city has thus become the *milieu par excellence* for the hellish activities that so significantly qualify human existence in a contemporary technological society.

For Simon's narrators, the inevitable fear of falling into this underworld is therefore analogous to what Gilbert Durand has termed "un rappel brutal de notre humaine et présente condition terrestre."[16]   Their use of mythological heroes and archetypal symbols translates ancient initiatory themes of torture and death in the underworld into modern images of human existence.   Not unlike Joyce's classical references in *Ulysses,*[17] the multiplicity of myths and archetypal symbols pertaining to the contemporary city in Simon's fiction do, in fact, perform the primary function of myth which has always been to create exemplary models for all of man's significant activities, persistent models that continue to reflect a primordial condition.

Flight Toward the Heavens

Surprisingly enough, all the disappointments of modern society, which seem to form the principle thematic backdrop for both *Histoire* and *La Bataille de Pharsale,* do not constrain each narrator's dream of poetic transcendence.   Desperate to free themselves from the monstrous presence of the city, they utilize symbols of flight or ascension toward the Heavens to juxtapose those of descent or entrapment in the labyrinthine underworld.   Ascension, whether real or imaginary, thereby expresses a significant ontological change, severing the narrators from the underworld in order that they may surpass or transcend that particular human condition.[18] This form of transcendence is never permanent, however, since upward and downward symbols constantly alternate in their narratives.

Birds play a prominent role in depicting each narrator's desire for levitation. For what could be more fundamentally ascensional than a bird in flight? "L'outil ascensionnel par excellence," affirms Durand, "c'est bien l'aile."[19] Consequently, the bird in flight is the most de-animalized of all animals in Simon's fiction, evoking the concepts of height and movement more often than the physical attributes of a specific organism. Birds in the Simonian text are frequently described as symbolic pairs of wings moving upward, toward freedom: "Disparu au-dessus des toits. Façon de parler: pas vu disparaître et pas vu réellement les toits. Simplement haut par opposition à bas. C'est-à-dire en bas un néant originel. . .en haut un autre néant, entre lesquels il s'est soudain matérialisé, un instant, ailes déployées, comme l'immobile figuration du concept même d'ascension, un instant, puis plus rien" (*BP*, 10). In this regard, Bachelard argues that a "force symbolique" of lightness, youth, and purity exists in the unconscious before creating the ascensional image of a bird in flight. These impressions provide us with our first psychic realities: "c'est parce que nous vivons par l'imagination un vol heureux, un vol qui nous donne l'impression de jeunesse, c'est parce que le vol onirique est souvent—contre toutes les leçons de la psychanalyse classique—une 'volupté' du 'pur' que nous donnons tant de qualités 'morales' à l'oiseau qui traverse le ciel de nos journées."[20]

In the course of merely two pages, the narrator in *Histoire* moves back and forth several times from descriptions of the commercial Spider-Woman to reflections on the birds outside in a furious attempt to escape entanglement in her mercantile net. The defiant cries of a pestered bird seem to translate his own inner torment: "Au bout d'un moment l'un d'eux [des oiseaux] réapparut perché sur l'angle du mur et du toit aiguisa son bec au bord de la tuile pencha la tête à gauche puis à droite puis lança de nouveau son cri bête strident" (*HI*, 230-231). Similar comparisons abound in all three novels. In several instances, the narrator in *La Bataille de Pharsale* associates birds with bows, arrows, and even javelins, as additional ascensional symbols. Though technological imitations of a natural phenomenon, they too express a rupture with the hellish existence on or below the surface of the earth: "non pas un oiseau mais seulement cette impression, déjà souvenir, de foudroyant montée, de foudroyante ascension verticale, et d'autre part, pour l'oeil, cette image d'arbalète, et alors la voûte de flèches, les traits volant dessinant une arche entre les deux armées" (*BP,* 42).   The straight and sudden movement of birds and arrows often carries the narrative consciousness toward the purity of the sun, away from the darkness of the underworld. It is no accident then, that *La Bataille de Pharsale,* the novel in which underworld imagery is most completely developed, should both open and close with these particular ascensional symbols: "jaune et puis noir temps d'un battement de paupières et puis jaune de nou-veau: ailes déployées forme d'arbalète rapide entre le soleil et l'oeil ténèbres un instant sur les visages comme un velours une main un instant ténèbres puis lumière" (*BP,* 9 and 271).   Ex-ploiting this same ascensional symbolism to its fullest, *Le Palace* concludes with two juxtaposing images: a flight of pigeons moving across a sunlit sky and, down below, an abandoned city whose subterranean corridors, like the palace of some forgotten queen, house the small black coffins of its own still-born children (*LP,* 229-230).   For Simon's narrators, it is as if the birds were celestial messengers, man's constant reminder of a world of light that lies upward and beyond the alternately bleak or garish laby-rinthine corridors of the modern metropolis.

Elevation confers power because it moves man, animal, and object alike closer to the sun and the celestial bodies, the great life-givers. And, as Neumann reminds us, "heaven is the dwelling place of gods and genii, symbolizing the world of light and consciousness as contrasted with the earthy, body-bound world of the unconscious."[21]   Hence an alliance with the luminous heavens provides the narrators with the possibility of transcen-dence. For this reason, the narrator in *La Bataille de Pharsale* is markedly moved by the semi-nude workers depicted on a foreign stamp who stretch their enchained wrists upward toward the sun-light in a symbolically liberating gesture (*BP,* 209).   For O., this ascensional movement of uplifted chains speaks of man's quest for freedom from the institutions that confine him far better than any revolutionary slogan. It is ironic, indeed, that man in the contemporary city has become a continual bird of prey for the civilization that he has helped to construct. When confronted with the perils of the archetypal city, the revolutionary quality of the Simonian hero lies in his conquest of fear and his aspiration toward the purity and light of another world which he can imagine, but never reach. "Quelque faiblesse qu'aient nos ailes imaginaires," asserts Bachelard, "la rêverie de vol nous ouvre un monde, elle est ouverture au monde, grande ouverture, large ouverture. Le ciel est la fenêtre du monde."[22]

Clearly in the tradition of the ancient mythological heroes, the central questions which concern Simon's narrators are those of initiation, death, and a rebirth of innocence. The modern city has become one of several initiatory arenas in which Simon's self-reflecting consciousness may discover itself through encounters with the surrounding environment. Monsters, even Hell itself, have no doubt altered their setting, but the contemporary heroic adventure is no less hazardous because it now takes place amid the banal preoccupations of a technologically advanced civilization. In fact, Neumann insists that traditionally, in the archaic as well as more modern societies, "mankind has projected one part of the archetypal 'inner' world into 'heaven,' and another part into 'Hell.'"[23] The ancient physical ordeals have simply given way to the psychological trials which constantly arise in the acutely mechanized communities of the 20th century. For the Simonian narrator, and perhaps for ourselves as well, confronting the infernal, labyrinthine qualities of the archetypal city has become one of the principle challenges of the modern era.

Mother Earth

Complementing their experiences in the archetypal city, initiatory journeys out into the world invite Simon's narrators to witness the foreboding grandeur of Mother Earth, where they learn of the perennial rhythms governing the natural world. Like Erich Neumann's Great Mother archetype, Mother Earth is both life-giver and cruel destroyer in Simon's fiction. Metaphorically speaking, the earth is primarily perceived as the great archetypal Feminine "because that which is contained, sheltered, nourished is dependent on it and utterly at its mercy."[24] As a Good Mother, she nourishes and calms, protects and keeps warm:

"au milieu de la route dans la sylvestre paix où je pouvais tou-
jours entendre les coucous et de temps en temps le rapide in-
visible et paresseux saut d'un poisson hors de l'inaltérable miroir
de l'eau" (*RF*, 164). In death, she may also function as a final
"berceau magique,"[25] calling man back to her protective womb
and assuaging his fears: "le visage parmi l'herbe nombreuse, la
terre velue, son corps tout entier aplati, comme s'il s'efforçait
de disparaître entre les lèvres du fossé, se fondre, se glisser, se
faufiler tout entier par cette étroite fissure pour réintégrer la
paisible matière (matrice) originelle" (*RF*, 244). More often
than not, however, Mother Earth emerges as a Terrible Mother
who torments or brutalizes her children and ultimately feeds
on their corpses with peaceful indifference: "sans le soleil la
campagne semblait encore plus morte abandonnée effrayante
par sa paisible et familière immobilité cachant la mort aussi
paisible aussi familière et aussi peu sensationnelle que les bois
les arbres les près fleuris" (*RF*, 92). As a result, Nature is never
more than a momentary and regrettably deceptive refuge for
Simon's narrators.

The principle attributes of the Simonian Mother Earth are
her indefatigable power and seemingly infinite expanse. Scholars
generally agree that in many myths and mystery religions the
initiatory ordeal begins with the separation of the neophyte
from his family, followed by a journey into a forest or an equiva-
lently mysterious terrain, since the forest, jungle, sea, or darkness
usually symbolize "the beyond."[26] Encountering the inter-
minable immensity of the natural world becomes a similarly
disturbing and oftentimes alienating experience for the narrative
consciousness in Simon's novels. The confused wanderings of the
soldiers in *La Route des Flandres,* which become one of the
novel's central motifs, appear in Simon's texts as early as *La
Corde raide* (1947) and as recently as *Leçon de choses* (1975),
depicting man's utter helplessness and insecurity in the expansive
world of Nature: "puis ils. . .furent de nouveau dehors, flottant
dans cette espèce de vastitude, de vacuité, de vide cotonneux,
entourés de tous côtés par le bruit ou plutôt la rumeur pour ainsi
dire tranquille de la bataille" (*RF*, 115). As the quotation sug-
gests, Georges apprehends the outside world as a kind of void, a
vacant sphere offering no stability for the self. And since the
search for wholeness is perhaps the foremost struggle in Simon's
novels, it is little wonder that, for the narrative consciousness,
Nature becomes one of the major obstacles to that end.

On many occasions, the boundless depths of the earth instill the narrators with a new sense of awe and humility. Like a vast forest or the darkness of night, the sea appears to encompass all of life in its silent breast like "le vide le néant sans haut ni bas ni ouverture" (*HI*, 320). The nephew's insistence on the word "ouverture" is, it seems, worth emphasizing for the sea, the forest, and the whole of the natural world silently encompass man throughout his life. If, then, the archetypal city is experienced as a monstrous cavern or a series of labyrinthine corridors, it is still less intimidating than Mother Earth by virtue of the fact than an opening always exists to the cavern or labyrinth. In Nature, however, there is never a permanent escape, merely varying degrees of successful shelters which may ostensibly seal man off from the natural world but which may never remove him entirely from Nature's grasp. Hence the perpetual fall of rain on the Flanders Road also gives a single, all-enveloping black color to the world, slowly gnawing away at all material, organic or otherwise, like an army of hungry ants: "la pluie commença à tomber, elle aussi monotone, infinie et noire, et non pas se déversant mais, comme la nuit elle-même, englobant dans son sein hommes et montures" (*RF*, 30). Closely resembling the pivotal role of the personified wind in *Le Vent* (1957), the rain, sea, and earth in *La Route des Flandres* intervene in human activity like capricious homeric gods. Acknowledging the physical predominance of these natural forces constitutes each narrator's first initiatoty step toward cognizance of the world picture.

The infinite in Nature is also the eternal, that which has no conceivable beginning or end but retains its own rhythmic order. In Simon's fiction, both the rain and the sea typify the timeless quality of Mother Earth, who never ceases to be, yet is always altering her appearance: "très loin dans le temps, ou de tous les temps, ou en dehors du temps, la pluie tombant toujours et peut-être depuis toujours" (*RF*, 64). As in many East Indian religions, the historic world, the world of civilizations commenced and ended, seems unreal when compared with the perennial cosmic rhythms.[27] The proof, for Georges, is that Nature covers over all the human debris of defeat on the Flanders Road in a year's time, no more than a brief instant in the earth's history: "après que tout avait pris fin, c'est-à-dire s'était refermé, cicatrisé, ou plutôt (pas cicatrisé, car aucune trace de ce qui s'était passé n'était déjà plus visible) rajusté, recollé, et si parfaitement qu'on ne pouvait plus discerner la moindre faille,

comme la surface de l'eau se referme sur un caillou" (*RF*, 232).
Like a mysterious surface filled with hidden depths, the earth
assimilates men and objects into her age-old folds without leav-
ing behind the slightest vestige of their existence.

Initiation to the laws of Nature thereby demands that the
individual consciousness submit to the terrestrial powers which
encompass all of life. In a very real sense, each narrator's self-
exploration in the natural world moves him toward a fuller
acceptance of his human subservience to the external environ-
ment. Georges, for example, feels impotent in relation to the
mighty powers of the earth and sea. Mercilessly exposed to the
elements during wartime, he is magnetically drawn back to the
earth, which he reluctantly recognizes as his place of origin and
final receptacle in death: "comme la couleur même de la guerre,
de la terre, s'emparant d'eux peu à peu, eux, leurs visages ter-
reux, leurs loques terreuses, leurs yeux terreux aussi, de cette
teinte sale, indistincte qui semblait les assimiler déjà à cette
argile, cette boue, cette poussière dont ils étaient sortis et à
laquelle, errants, honteux, hébétés et tristes, ils retournaient
chaque jour un peu plus" (*RF*, 172). Even the poetic devices in
this passage emphasize the significance of the earth's power over
men at war: notice, for example, the riming of terre/guerre/
terreux/errants, the repetition of terreux/terreuses in slightly
altered rhymthic patterns and the dramatic visual breakdown of
"terre" into "cette argile, cette boue, cette poussière." The de-
composing horse alongside the Flanders Road engenders a like
comparison as the earth slowly ushers in its process of transmuta-
tion and reassimilation: "à moitié absorbé semblait-il par la
terre, comme si celle-ci avait déjà sournoisement commencé à
reprendre possession de ce qui était issu d'elle, n'avait vécu que
par sa permission et son intermédiaire" (*RF*, 27). In this way,
Mother Earth marks each organism's journey through life from
beginning to end, ultimately taking "everything that is born of it
back into its womb of origination and death."[28]

The initiatory ordeal in Nature may also pit the self against
a thoroughly malefic cosmos. The murder or possible suicide
of Captain de Reixach, a leit-motif that appears in both *La Route
des Flandres* and *Histoire,* points toward the quiet complicity of
Nature in human slaughter: "comme si la nature tout entière
complice des assassins se retenait de respirer dans l'attente du
meurtre, s'était soudain mués en quelque chose d'à la fois in-

différent et perfide" (*HI*, 190). In such instances, death is no longer simply a case of life returning to its place of origin, but the willful destruction of man, beast, and object by the lurking forces of Mother Earth. One such example in *La Route des Flandres* is the insidious rain that gradually, but nevertheless wantonly, dissolves everything in its path. Merging with the monotonous sounds of horse hooves on the war-torn battle road, the falling rain becomes a ruthless accomplice in widespread death and destruction: "ce froid cette eau qui maintenant nous pénétraient de toutes parts, ce même ruissellement obstiné multiple omniprésent qui se mélangeait semblait ne faire qu'un avec l'apocalyptique le multiple piétinement des sabots sur la route" (*RF*, 277). The fusion here, of natural and human forces of destruction is reminiscent of the biblical passage in which God's apocalyptic prophecy fortells of how man shall fight his brother while pestilence, overflowing rain, fire, and brimstone torment him.[29] The recurrent image of the four lost soldiers who wander in search of their army further develops the biblical vision of the Four Horsemen of the Apocalypse who represent Conquest, War, Famine, and Death: "cette ville où il n'y avait plus rien que cette lamentable procession de fourmis et nous quatre sur nos rosses fourbues" (*RF*, 309). While contemplating a Roman frieze, the narrator in *La Bataille de Pharsale* makes a parallel reference to these same four cavalry men: "le soleil, la pluie, le gel, la nuit, les aubes, les jours passent tour à tour sur eux sans que leur course se ralentisse" (*BP*, 263-264). This, then, is the veritable spectre of the modern apocalypse when Nature and History join forces in a combined and unrelenting effort to ravage man and environment alike.

"En s'exprimant par des images matérielles, par des images terrestres," notes Bachelard, "il semble que les peines humaines deviennent plus lourdes, plus noires, plus dures, plus troubles, bref, plus réelles. Le réalisme terrestre est alors une surcharge."[30] Surely, this is the case for Simon's narrators, whose imagery reflects a primitive dread of Nature's role in the death and dissolution of living matter. Yet by far the most distressing characteristic of Mother Earth is her callous indifference to this destructive process: " 'le massacre aussi bien que l'amour est un prétexte à glorifier la forme dont la splendeur calme apparaît seulement à ceux qui ont pénétré l'indifférence de la nature devant le massacre et l'amour' " (*BP*, 119). Forgetful and unconcerned, the earth absorbs all life in order to replenish itself

and give birth again. A rusty, abandoned machine rots incon-
spicuously as the earth quietly repossesses it, "sans que personne
se soit approché de la machine et sans que le vent souffle, l'une
des extrémités d'une tringle se détache et tombe sur le sol. . .
Celui-ci est à demi rempli de terre et de sable apportés par le
vent et fixés par les pluies. Le choc a été amorti par les herbes
qui ont possé là. Le bruit a été imperceptible" (*BP*, 244). By
extension, the comings and goings of human life, like those of
battered machines and decaying cities, are equally insignificant
in the eyes of Mother Earth.

Initiation to Nature thereby reveals the inconsequentiality
of individual life and death when staged against a larger cosmic
backdrop. Even the tremendous losses incurred at Verdun in the
summer of 1914 seem of little import when incorporated into
the natural cycle of events: "ce n'était toujours que le même et
unique paysage à l'aspect uniforme de décharge publique, hérissé
non de pattes de chevaux morts mais de poutres cassées, de
ferrailles, d'échardes, et chaotique" (*HI*, 105). For despite the
massive scale of such a disaster, human deaths do not effect the
rhythmic constancy of the natural order. Consequently, Georges
imagines that his own death could in no way scar or even mea-
surably mark the surrounding countryside: "qu'est-ce qu'il y
aurait de changé sinon qu'il ne serait plus tout à fait dans la
même position puisqu'il aurait essayé d'épauler et viser, et c'était
tout, car en définitive ce serait toujours la même paisible et tiède
soirée de mai avec sa verte senteur d'herbe et la légère humidité
bleuâtre qui commençait à tomber sur les vergers et les jardins"
(*RF*, 246). Aside from the cold-blooded, chaotic fury of Mother
Earth, there is a kind of Ovidian naturel order here, to which the
narrators ultimately submit. This submission to the powers that
have always controlled man's rites of passage through the domain
of Nature is an essential part of the modern initiatory process.
To pursue an identity, the narrators must become cognizant
of those forces which continue to challenge and even limit their
human aspirations. Although destined to annihilation, they con-
sole themselves with the realization that they too participate in
the larger cyclic process of life, death, and regeneration, which
Ovid describes with delicate simplicity in *The Metamorphoses:*

'Nothing retains the shape of what it was,
And Nature, always making old things new,
Proves nothing dies within the universe,

But takes another being in new forms.
What is called birth is change from what we were,
And death the shape of being left behind,
Though all things melt or grow from here to there,
Yet the same balance of the world remains.'[31]

The Shelter

Responding to the dangers of Nature, which always threaten to castrate the individual free will, the narrative consciousness in many of Simon's novels often chooses to retreat from the world "outside," moving "inward" in serach of some shelter for the self. As in the archetypal city, so in Nature, rites of liberation follow periods of initiatory submission. Flight toward the Heavens and withdrawal into the self are comparable forms of deliverance from the external forces which continually menace the psyche. To counter the anguish of solitude and impotence in the world outside, Simon's narrators, like Proust's Marcel, cling to the stability of objects and shelters in the hope of securing some fixity in the world. This attempt at self-stabilization occurs because, as in Proust and more recently in Nathalie Sarraute and Alain Robbe-Grillet, "the being that is uncertain of himself wants to lean upon the stability of things."[32]

In the continually transmuting world of Nature, the narrators and the phenomena around them appear as victims of an everchanging present. The results is that they experience life as an eternally fluid process which closely resembles the countryside viewed from a passing train. "le monde n'apparaît à aucun instant identique à ce qu'il était dans l'instant qui l'a immédiatement précédé" (*BP*, 186). Although stability is never wholly tenable, each narrator pursues it in various forms, one of which involves the search for a fixed enclosure. The narrators' fascination with trains moving tirelessly outward, "into space," in both *Histoire* and *La Bataille de Pharsale* is due primarily to the solidity the train provides for its passengers: "le vaste monde couché sous les nuages suspendus Coupant noir rigide et métallique à travers les champs les vallées les forêts. . .emporté immobile sur cette banquette" (*BP*, 163). The train's firm iron walls seem to anchor the narrator in something of permanence, enabling his mind to meander freely within the contours of a solid physical space. And as Françoise Van Rossum-Guyon has already demonstrated, the train compartment furnishes an analogously stable construct for Michel Butor's narrator in *La Modification*.[33]

Shelters also function in another capacity in Simon's novels as a type of centering agent for the self, protecting it from the hostilities that accumulate outside. The house, Bachelard observes, "est un instrument à affronter le cosmos."[34] A country dwelling on the Flanders Road supplies Georges with his only weapon against the apocalyptic fury of Mother Earth who has formed a catastrophic alliance with human warfare. This house serves as a purely physical protection: "c'était de n'être plus dehors, d'avoir quatre murs autour de soi, et un plafond au-dessus de la tête" (*RF*, 112). Likewise, for the narrator in *Histoire*, the warmth of his family house protected people and plants from the bitter cold of Nature's winters: "Certains hivers les cimes gelaient mais tout ce qui était à l'abri de la maison était protégé" (*HI*, 98). Ironic as it may seem, even the prison building in *La Route des Flandres* appears to shield its captives from the still more dreadful world beyond its boundaries much the way the asylum protects the inmates in Beckett's *Malone meurt*.

In the opening pages of *Histoire*, the narrator is in bed, reminiscing over certain early childhood experiences which may be interpreted as key memories from an elusive past. He remembers trying to see his mother's dying body through the proliferation of flowers and people surrounding her bed: "un instant j'avais pu voir aussi ou plutôt entrevoir le visage de maman sur les oreillers" (*HI*, 16). It is as if these visual obstacles represented all the years and events that now separate the narrator from the deceased maternal figure. His desire to move through the above-mentioned obstacles, toward his mother, translates a symbolic need to return to his place of origin. Indeed, this search for origins, which is a prominent theme in many of Simon's novels, appropriately takes place in the narrator's childhood house. It is there that the narrator shuffles through his mother's old post cards in an attempt to piece together the fragmented impressions he has retained of his parents in the years of their courtship and brief marriage. The parental house invites a search for self-identity because, as Bachelard has argued, it constitutes the narrator's first universe.[35]

The more intimate the enclosure, the more conducive it is to rediscovering a center of stability or of personal roots amid confusion and intimidation from the exterior. In Simon's fictional world, the narrative consciousness most frequently confronts daydreams, memories, and mental obsessions, which are the internal forces at work in the psyche, from within the confines of an enclosed space. Georges, for instance, remembers his past in a hotel room, the nephew in *Histoire* mulls over childhood remembrances in his mother's house, and O. attempts to collect and solidify his scattered impressions of self while working at the desk in his study, self-consciously writing *La Bataille de Pharsale*. In this way, a house or room shelters not only their physical being, but more important no doubt, their psychic being. "La maison," Bachelard concludes, "est une des plus grandes puissances d'intégration pour les pensées, les ouvenirs et les rêves de l'homme. . .La maison, dans la vie de l'homme, évince des contingences, elle multiplie ses conseils de continuité. Sans elle, l'homme serait un être dispersé. Elle maintient l'homme à travers les orages du ciel et les orages de la vie."[36] *L'Herbe* tends to give credence to Bachelard's assertion since what we might call the magnetism of the notion of "home" is, finally, the most compelling image for Louise, despite a desire to loose herself in Nature.

Regardless of its particular characteristics, the intimate spatial enclosure acts as a protector and synthesizer of the narrators' initiatory experiences and personal reveries. Hence the creative act of writing itself, which happens "inside," is an attempt to give some unity to the narrator's pespective on the world, however chaotic that unity may appear at first glance. Nevertheless, a unifying perspective is possible only after Simon's narrators have come to terms with the external, as well as the internal worlds of the human cirucumstance. But the real treasure of this synthetic process is a rediscovered sense of wholeness, which the narrators strive to secure despite the inevitable failure of that project, and which "lies buried in the most intimate parts of our own house; that is, of our own being. It is behind the stove, the centre of the life and warmth that rule our existence, the heart of our heart, if only we knew how to unearth it. And yet—there is this strange and persistent fact, that it is only after a pious journey in a distant region, in a new land, that the meaning of that inner voice guiding us on our search can make itself understood by us."[37]

Little by little, then, initiatory rites of passage in the world "outside" inform Simon's narrators of the unrestrainable forces at work in Nature and of the security to be found in a protective enclosure. Like their primitive ancestors, each narrator is led to acknowledge his own physical frailty and inevitable fate by submitting to these cosmic powers. Whether it be in Nature, in the city, with Woman, or on the battlefield, establishing an orientation in the world is critical in Simon's fiction since man knows himself only through encounters with his environment. However fluctuating his world may appear, the narrator's search for self automatically calls into question the essential state of things in that world. To that end, Mother Earth provides him with a number of archetypal patterns which organize and mold the whole of what he determines to be the human condition.

In all of the archetypal scenarios we have examined thus far, universal behavioral responses emerge from what may first look like a totally chaotic universe in which incidents occur or do not occur entirely by chance. Although this element of chance remains one of the principle agents at work in the cosmos, it is not, as one critic has argued,[38] the single driving force that gives shape to Simon's world. Whereas chance determines what is unique in the individual, the archetypal situations encountered in love, war, Nature, and society delineate what is universal in the life process of the Simonian hero. Individuality and universality do, in fact, effectively merge through each narrator's continued use of imagistic patterns which refer to specific myths and archetypes. Their imagery suggests that "at the center of the experience of individuality is the realization that all other individuals share the same experience as ourselves of living in a single, sealed world, and that this realization connects us meaningfully with all other units of life. The result," a contemporary Jungian concludes, "is that we do experience ourselves as part of a continuum."[39] Indeed, it seems likely that Simon would agree with Hans Meyerhoff's hope that "by recognizing ourselves in the mythical image of past struggles, triumphs, and defeats of man, we may also come to reconcile ourselves to the inescapable limitations imposed, by Nature and society, upon the human condition now and at all times."[40]

Clearly, one of the primary functions of mythological and archetypal imagery in Simon's work *is* to emphasize the perennial nature of man's initiatory odyssey into the unknown, whether that be the battlefield, Nature, a feminine figure, or the very city in which he lives. Each narrator's schematization of a personal journey through life profoundly relates an archaic past to a not altogether chaotic present which continues to echo those eternal configurations that have persisted throughout History.

NOTES

[1]Maurice Merleau-Ponty, "What is Phenomenology" in *European Literary Theory and Practice,* trans. by Colin Smith, ed. by Vernon W. Gras (New York: Dell, 1973), p. 73.

[2]Nature is referred to in this chapter with a capital "N" because, as the discussion will suggest, it is indeed perceived as an active and personified force with which man must reckon.

[3]See Georges Gusdorf's discussion of mythic and rational conceptions of space in *Mythe et métaphysique* (Paris: Flammarion, 1953).

[4]Eisenstein's concept of montage is based on a theory of the conflicting or contrasting juxtaposition of film images. This montage process can be characterized, he argues, "by the conflict of two pieces in opposition to each other. By conflict. By collision." See Sergei Eisenstein's "The Cinematographic Principle and the Ideogram" in *Film Form,* ed. and trans. by Jay Leyda (New York: World, 1957), p. 37.

[5]Mircea Eliade, *Myth and Reality,* trans. by Willard R. Trask (New York: Harper and Row, 1968), p. 141.

[6]Mircea Eliade, *Myths, Dreams, and Mysteries,* trans. by Philip Mairet (1957; rept. New York: Harper and Row, 1960), p. 200.

[7]Gilbert Durand, *Les Structures anthropologiques de l'imaginaire* (Paris: Bordas, 1969), p. 227.

[8]*Ibid.,* pp. 123-124.

[9]Gaston Bachelard, *L'Air et les songes* (Paris: Corti, 1943), p. 108.

[10]Eliade, *Myths, Dreams, and Mysteries,* pp. 222-223. Eliade also discusses at length the notion of initiatory death and rebirth in *Rites and Symbols of Initiation,* trans. by Willard R. Trask (1958; rpt. New York:

Harper and Row, 1965).

[11]Northrop Frye, *Anatomy of Criticism* (Princeton: Princeton University Press,1971), p. 150.

[12]See Eliade's *Rites and Symbols of Initiation,* and Erich Neumann's *The Great Mother,* trans. by Ralph Manheim (1955; rpt. Princeton: Princeton University Press, 1972).

[13]Neumann, *The Great Mother,* p. 177.

[14]Erich Neumann, *The Origins and History of Consciousness,* trans. by R. F. C. Hull (1949; rpt. Princeton: Princeton University Press, 1971), p. 162.

[15]Durand, *Les Structures anthropologiques de l'imaginaire,* p. 116. Durand refers to Rank's interpretation found in *Traumatisme de la naissance* (Paris: Payot, 1928), p. 30.

[16]*Ibid.,* p. 124.

[17]R. M. Albérès has argued, rather unconvincingly I believe, that Simon's novels lack the symbolic, transhistorical dimension found in a great modern mythmaker such as Joyce. He concludes that in *Histoire,* "aucun de ces épisodes de la plus grande banalité ne prend une valeur mythique comme chez Joyce, ni même une très forte puissance lyrique." I can only surmise that Albérès, like so many others, has failed to distinguish between a work that renarrates one particular classical myth and a novel, like *Histoire,* which contains fragmentary mythological motifs that cannot be traced through the whole narrative. Though different techniques, both approaches may, in fact, awaken us to the archetypal patterns which frame the essence of our human experiences. See R. M. Albérès, *Le Roman d'aujourd'hui,* 1960-1970 (Paris: Albin Michel, 1970), p. 245.

[18]In *Myths, Dreams, and Mysteries,* p. 106, Eliade argues that the symbolisms of flight and ascension "express a break with the universe of everyday experience."

[19]Durand, *Les Structures anthropologiques de l'imaginaire,* p. 144.

[20]Bachelard, *L'Air et les songes,* p. 83.

[21]Neumann, *The Origins and History of Consciousness,* p. 311.

[22]Gaston Bachelard, *La Poétique de la rêverie* (Paris: PUF, 1968), p. 180.

[23]Neumann, *The Great Mother,* p. 40.

[24]*Ibid.,* p. 43.

[25]Durand, *Les Structures anthropologiques de l'imaginaire,* p. 270.

[26]Eliade, *Myths, Dreams, and Mysteries,* pp. 197-198.

[27]Mircea Eliade, *Images and Symbols,* trans. by Philip Mairet (1952; rpt. New York: Sheed and Ward, 1969), p. 68.

[28]Neumann, *The Great Mother,* p. 30.

[29]*The Oxford Annotated Bible: The Holy Bible,* Revised Standard Version, ed. by Herbert G. May and Bruce M. Metzger (New York: Oxford University Press, 1962), Ezekiel, pp, 38, 20-22.

[30]Gaston Bachelard, *La Terre et les rêveries de la volonté* (Paris: Corti, 1948), p. 128.

[31]Ovid, *The Metamorphoses,* ed. by Horace Gregory (New York: Viking, 1958), p. 430.

[32]Georges Poulet, *Studies in Human Time,* trans. by Elliott Coleman (Baltimore: John Hopkin's Press, 1956), p. 293.

[33]For a more detailed discussion of both Time and Space in Butor's novel, see Françoise Van Rossum-Guyon's *Critique du roman* (Paris: Gallimard, 1970).

[34]Gaston Bachelard, *La Poétique de l'espace* (Paris: PUF, 1972), p. 58.

[35]*Ibid.,* p. 24.

[36]*Ibid.,* p. 26.

[37]This quotation from Heinrich Zimmer is cited by Eliade in *Myths, Dreams, and Mysteries,* p. 245.

[38]John Sturrock states in *The French New Novel* (London: Oxford University Press, 1969), p. 70, that the central theme running throughout Simon's fiction is the recognition that chance determines all existence.

[39]Edward F. Edinger, *Ego and Archetype* (Baltimore: Penguin, 1973), p. 178.

[40]Hans Meyerhoff, *Time in Literature* (Berkeley: University of California Press, 1968), p. 82.

IV

MYTH AND HISTORY

In the preceding chapters we have uncovered and examined those behavioral characteristics and common human situations in three of Simon's novels that seem to repeat themselves throughout time and which we may therefore refer to as "archetypal" configurations or perhaps describe even more simply as intuitive insights capable of bridging the gap between modern man and his archaic ancestors. Whether consciously or unconsciously inspired, such perennial patterns establish an imperishable order which in some measure speaks to as well as reveals the ultimate mysteries of the universe. For Jung and for more recent myth critics, mythological motifs and archetypes function as a powerful ordering principle because "he who speaks in primordial images speaks with a thousand voices; he enthralls and overpowers, while at the same time he lifts the idea he is trying to express out of the occasional and the transitory into the realm of the ever-enduring. He transmutes our personal destiny into the destiny of mankind, thereby evoking in us all those beneficient forces that ever and anon have enabled mankind to find a refuge from every peril and to outlive the longest night."[1]

The survival of these archetypal symbols within the modern psyche has much to say about our envisagement of the temporal sphere. Simon's conception of Time and what it indicates about man's relationship to the historical world, past, present, and future, needs further consideration in order to determine the nature of the rapport that exists between the Simonian man and History. . For, as Eliade reminds us, it is "by analysing the attitude of the modern man towards Time that we can penetrate the disguises of his mythological behavior."[2] The analysis that follows will survey and evaluate responses to the temporal rhythms and laws that govern the lives of Simon's protagonists and continue to shape the general human situation.

The Passage of Time

Because of its "obsessional" recurrence, the irreversible passage of Time is probably the single most significant theme in *L'Herbe, La Route des Flandres, Le Palace, Histoire,* and *La Bataille de Pharsale.* Kierkegaard and more recent existential thinkers have uniquely shown how man's growing awareness of himself gives rise to a beforehand knowledge of his eventual death. Deprived of the firm religious convictions of his ancestors, modern man more particularly senses a connection between Time and death, which is one of the primary reasons for his anxiety about being in the world. As one contemporary critic has put it: "Les hommes du XXe xiècle, parce qu'ils sont de moins en moins solitaires, sont justement de plus en plus seuls. Toutes les proies s'évanouissent entre leurs mains; au milieu de tant de bruit, c'est encore le temps qu'ils entendent; et à travers tant de visages, dont la transparence n'arrête pas leurs regards, c'est toujours la mort qu'ils aperçoivent, comme la seule réalité, la seule évidence, la seule chose vivante en ce monde."[3] In Simon's fiction, this existential revelation leads, in turn, to the recognition that life and death are inextricably intertwined and that, as Leonardo's paradoxical reflection suggests, to know life one must also come to know death. "Je croyais apprendre à vivre, j'apprenais à mourir,"[4] becomes the skeletal thematic framework around which many of Simon's novels unfold, a framework in which the Simonian hero views not only war, but life itself as a vast apprenticeship for death. Like Beckett's aimless characters, Simon's narrators are fully rooted in the absurdist tradition of the 20th century that accentuates the solitary nature of the human experience and simultaneously depicts man's utter powerlessness over his ultimate destiny.

Insofar as it signifies an unalterable movement toward death, destruction, and decay, the flow of Time in Simon's fiction carries with it a foreboding message. *La Route des Flandres, Histoire,* and *La Bataille de Pharsale* are impregnated from beginning to end with the fleeting images of men, animals, and objects in decay. Georges relives his first confrontations with death through a series of recurrent memories that deal primarily with: dying horses alongside the Flanders Road, Captain de Reixach's futile gestures when ambushed, Wack's surprised expression in death, the ancestral portrait couched in an unresolved mystery of suicide, and Georges' own bewilderment at being alive after falling unconscious on the battlefield. He remembers, too, how Time appeared to accelerate in battle because the crucial question of life or death was ever-present. Man, beast, and machine alike were constantly exposed to elements which continued a process of cold-blooded destruction even after death: "as-tu remarqué comme tout cela va vite, cette espèce d'accélération du temps, d'extraordinaire rapidité avec laquelle la guerre produit des phénomènes—rouille, souillures, ruines, corrosion des corps— qui demandent en temps ordinaire des mois ou des années pour s'accomplir?" (*RF,* 205). Hoping to end his contemporary military adventures in chivalrous triumph by capturing a beautiful modern princess, Georges found only an ugly old woman whose hideous deformities symbolically revealed Time's eventual conquest of even the loveliest maiden: "moi le cavalier le conquérant botté venu chercher au fond de la nuit au fond du temps séduire enlever la liliale princesse dont j'avais rêvé depuis des années et au moment où je croyais l'atteindre, la prendre dans mes bras, les refermant, enserrant, me trouvant face à face avec une horrible et goyesque vieille" (*RF,* 267). In Georges' eyes, the old woman is the antithesis, the complete corruption of his very concept of femininity embodied in the grace, voluptuousness, and above all else, in the radiance and exuberance of youth. In the presence of this new mock princess, Georges senses the ominous aura of death that also mirrors his own destiny.

For the narrators in *Histoire* and *La Bataille de Pharsale,* the mother, grandmother, elderly female relatives, and soldiers at war become the principle envoys of death. Moreover, the narrator's memory of his dying mother, so heavily drugged with morphine as to appear somnambulistic, dominates the mental associations and psychological meanderings throughout a major portion of *Histoire.* As death's archetypal victim, his mother represents the suffering multitudes of the past, present, and future who continue to hope for a miraculous recovery: "comme si quelque chose dans son destin l'avait irrésistiblement vouée à ces multitudes terribles et migratrices tourbillonnant sans fin à la surface de la terre errant de l'Orient à l'Occident à travers le

temps et l'espace. . .dans l'espoir d'impossibles miracles se
traînant claudiquant véhiculés dans un bruit de béquilles de
voitures d'infirmes" (*HI,* 226). A corpse-like figure walking
the tightrope between life and death, his mother's appearance
engenders only one question from her entourage, a question
about the time that is left: "le problème étant combien de
temps un organisme vivant peut-il continuer à fonctionner
lorsqu'il reste sur les os un simple sac de peau" (*HI,* 77). But
the narrator recognizes that all those who encircle her emaciated
body are themselves waiting for death and as a result, his de-
scriptions of them are particularly Proustian in both content and
perspective.   Like Marcel, he imagines them as queer, flaccid
shadows awaiting their own disappearance or perhaps already
dead without realizing it.

Likewise, O. envisions his grandmother with her deformed
fingers and old woman smell as the very embodiment of the
concept of death: "la vieille femme . . .dont l'aspect physique,
les vêtements et la fragilité avaient été si longtemps associés pour
moi à l'idée même de cadavre et de mort" (*BP,* 124). All three
narrators are acutely sensitive to the relentless march of Time
that takes the shape of a progressively expanding glacier as it
moves imperceptibly forward, slowly destroying everything in
its path: "cette olympienne et froide progression, ce lent glacier
en marche depuis le commencement des temps" (*RF,* 279).
Their awareness of Time's continual death toll appears to be
rooted in memories of their early family years when they either
witnessed or were told of the death of relatives. Once exposed
to the presence of death, they were forced to confront their own
life and mortality because, as Minkowski explains it, each death
"is a primitive *memento mori* for those who survive. I am
mortal not because I imagine I will be destined to disappear one
day, just as my fellow men disappear all around me, but because,
capable of registering death, I can do this only to the extent that
I carry death in me and because I am in this way identical with
my fellow men."[5] It is the haunting discovery of man's temporal
finitude, coupled with a sense of curiosity and horror about its
significance, that provides one of the essential thematic under-
pinnings for Simon's novels. His narrators acknowledge Time as
the great modern god who moves independent of all men and al-
ways leaves the victor.

Although unpredictable in its duration, the progression of a life toward death is irreversible in the Simonian world. Man, nature, and objects are similarly affected, gradually splintering, cracking, then falling to pieces like the aging photos, family portraits, and sculptures that populate each work: "apparemment intacts pourtant encore et en réalité en train de se décomposer à toute vitesse comme si sous la surface gisée et polie semblable à du marbre travaillait s'acharnait un invisible et vorace grouillement de sorte que peu à peu il ne resterait plus d'eux qu'une enveloppe illusoire une mince coque de plus en plus tenue" (*HI*, 359). As a result, the narrators perceive man to be a prisoner of Time, marooned on a continuously shrinking island, not unlike Ionesco's disintegrating palace in *Le Roi se meurt*, where there is no longer any hope of rescue. And as the last profoundly Proustian line of *La Route des Flandres* suggests, the island itself is not spared the destructive course of Time: "le monde arrêté figé s'effritant se dépiautant s'écroulant peu à peu par morceaux comme une bâtisse abandonnée, inutilisable, livrée à l'incohérent, nonchalant, impersonnel et destructeur travail du temps" (*RF*, 314).

Man oftentimes fights back in the face of his inevitable end by attempting to ignore, flee, or cover up the ravages of Time. According to Alan Harrington, "the immortality hunter searches unendingly for whatever means he can find to get around death. This involves manipulating his imagination to ignore nothingness or rise above it."[6] In Simon's novels it is primarily the women who wage the most vehement protests against the passage of Time by repressing the notion of death through family traditions and physical accoutrements. Georges' mother, for example, clings desperately to the remote aristocratic heritage on her mother's side of the family in order to give herself a sense of continuity in Time, while wearing more and more distinctly youthful apparel in seeming defiance of her aging body: "la flamboyante chevelure orange, les doigts endiamantés, les robes trop voyantes qu'elle s'obstinait à porter non malgré son âge, mais, semblait-il, en raison directement proportionnelle à celui-ci, le nombre, l'éclat, la violence des couleurs augmentant en même temps que le nombre des années" (*RF*, 52). In a similar protest, both the mother and the grandmother in *La Bataille de Pharsale* travel to Lourdes in the hope of benefiting from the sacred ceremonies and presumably health-restoring water.

Even Corinne, the remarkably sensuous cousin in *Histoire*

becomes yet another tracked animal, uselessly denying the mortality of her own body with a desperate profusion of jewels and silks in the hopes that this new artificial glitter can replace the lost sparkle of natural beauty: "la même surabondance, le même trop-plein de bijoux, de fards, de paroles, comme elles font toutes quand ça commence à les abandonner et qu'elles cherchent par quoi elles pourraient bien y remédier, essayent de remplacer l'éclat de leur peau, de leur chair, de leurs yeux par des éclats de voix, de scintillements métalliques ou de bouts de verre" (*HI*, 156). Then too, the quarrelsome sounds of hungry birds outside permeate the narrator's aging family house like the haunting objections to death made by the old made-up women who once filled its salons and ballroom.

Psychoanalysis argues that the acceptance of death, which—in Freudian terms—elicits the healthy reunification of Eros and the death instinct, occurs only through the abolition of repression.[7]   In general, however, Simon's women are too enmeshed in elaborately constructed denial systems to assimilate death into their own visions of the life process. And in so doing, they engage in the most serious kind of self-deception by attempting to evade the full impact of the passage of Time that confirms the mortality of the human mind and body; the essence of their world view is thus a refusal of reality.

Exposure to death is one of the fundamental steps in life's initiatory process in the Simonian text because it introduces his narrators to the concept of an individuated life, for "it is only in the presence of death that we come into contact in such an intimate manner with the notion of 'a' life."[8] With the death of someone else, the familiar, comfortable, even lovable aspects of their previous surroundings disappear, causing the narrators to register both a physical and psychological loss due to the termination of a life. This new sense of loss stems from the discontinuation of another being, an event that jars their own continuity in Time by depriving them of customary points of contact. It is for this reason that even the deaths of individuals with whom they felt little or no emotional attachment still mark their lives in disquieting ways by underscoring the unequivocal transience of all things: "comme si les invités, les ténébreuses vieilles reines, les jeunes filles aux bras nus, suaves, les musiciens, et même les portraits accrochés aux murs participaient d'un monde irréel en train de se décomposer, s'effriter, s'en aller en morceaux autour de ce cadavre vivant à la têtc fardéc, paréc, immobilisée" (*HI*, 62).   Thus, the approaching death of the narrator's mother in *Histoire* prefigures the disappearance and extinction of the people and objects immediately surrounding her. Simon's protagonists experience an ontological insecurity when confronted with their own lack of duration in Time; they imagine themselves as a substanceless liquid: "quelque chose de fluide, translucide et sans consistance réelle comme nous le sommes d'ailleurs tous plus ou moins dans le présent" (*HI*, 173). Their anguish resembles that of the modern existential hero condemned to a world without God and incapable of finding anything which might assure a continuation of his being.   The haunting question put forth by Camus also becomes their own: "est-ce que je cède au temps avare, aux arbres nus, à l'hiver du monde?"[9] Yet their post-existential trauma lies in their apparent inability to discover any course of action that might render their finite, individual life meaningful, or at the very least, comprehensible.

A Search for Duration

Since each narrator's relationship to Time is so closely tied to his concept of self, both organic and psychological, he feels compelled to find a stable center of awareness by establishing a sense of duration in the world.   If such a project cannot be achieved in the present moment because of a progressively menacing movement toward death, then another temporal dimension must be pursued in order to assure self-continuity.   The need to remove ourselves from the intimidations of present time is a common form of refuge in our daily lives as well as in literature. Powerless over the irreversible passage of Time and horrified by future prospects of their impending death, Simon's narrators retreat into the past in search of a more stable basis for being in the world.   Their search for self-clarification leads them to journey backward across their earlier lives in the hope of uncovering a fixed image of self.   As in *A la recherche du temps perdu,* their quest is to arrest the flow of physical time by recapturing a fundamental wholeness rooted presumably in their particular pasts.   This emphasis on and keen interest in the rediscovery of a lost self by rebuilding the past closely resembles the abiding principles of psychoanalytic therapy.[10] To be sure, both processes represent a mnemonic approach to life: for the narrator and the psychoanalyst, the construction of a durable notion of self demands an awareness of the past since the self is considered to be the sum of that past.

Although many stimuli remind the narrators of previous experiences, there is often a core situation or tight nucleus of events in the present which serves as an initial and oftentimes recurrent springboard for their odysseys into the past. Corinne, the widow of Georges' regiment captain in World War II, is the mediating bond linking past to present in *La Route des Flandres.* Lying next to Georges in a somber hotel room, Corinne's very presence seems to carry him backward in Time to those war memories and fantasies in which she played so vital a role: "non pas la lourde et poussiéreuse senteur du foin desseché, de l'été aboli, mais cette impalpable, nostalgique et tenance exhalaison du temps lui-même, des années mortes, et lui flottant dans les ténèbres, écoutant le silence, la nuit, la paix, l'imperceptible respiration d'une femme à côté de lui" (*RF*, 42). Because Georges consciously or unconsciously desires this temporal displacement, Corinne's physical proximity helps him effectively review isolated moments from his past: "Et il me semblait y être, voir cela" (*RF*, 19), or later, "Et cette fois Georges put les voir, exactement comme si lui-même avait été là" (*RF*, 144). His memories and reveries capture the chaotic defeat along the Flanders Road, the mean existence of prison life, the curiously enigmatic nature of de Reixach's murder and his ancestor's suicide, and even earlier interpersonal exchanges with his parents. Corinne relates to all of these episodes from his past not only because of her marriage to Captain de Reixach, but also and perhaps more important, because she somehow symbolizes the feminine ideal of sensuality, beauty, and coquettishness that both tortured and inspired him as well as others during long hours of despair on the battlefield and in prison. Reminiscent of Proust's Albertine, Corinne provides that mysterious link with the past like a "magicienne me présentant un miroir du temps."[11]

Yet in her own way, Corinne seems to recognize the abstract ideal that she has become for Georges, an ideal against which she must rebel, however flattering it might first appear.

When Georges insists on the depth of his long-standing love and desire for her over a period of five years, Corinne cynically retorts that she is a mere sexual object in his eyes: "il me semble qu'il n'est pas très difficile de se figurer à quoi peuvent penser pendant cinq ans un tas d'hommes privés de femmes, à peu près quelque chose dans le genre de ce qu'on voit dessiné sur les murs des cabines téléphoniques ou des toilettes des cafés je pense que c'est normal je pense que c'est la chose la plus naturelle mais dans ces sortes de dessins on ne représente jamais les figures" (*RF*, 96). Georges fights her interpretation primarily because he refuses to give up an ideal image that links him with a past to which he so desperately clings for security and continuity. Since duration, rather than Corinne, is Georges' principal obsession, he sees in his idealized version of her the means with which to recollect the essence of a historical self lost in Time.

Halting the present march of Time by anamnesis has a potentially consoling effect on all of Simon's narrators, for, as Durand explains, "bien loin d'être aux ordres du temps, la mémoire permet un redoublement des instants, et un dédoublement du présent; elle donne une épaisseur inusitée au morne et fatal écoulement du devenir, et assure dans les fluctuations du destin la survie et la pérennité d'une substance. Ce qui fait que le regret est toujours pénétré de quelque douceur et débouche tôt ou tard sur le remords. Car la mémoire, permettant de revenir sur le passé, autorise en partie la réparation des outrages du temps."[12] And so it is that in memory, as in fantasy and dream, Georges tries to evade a progressive temporal awareness by denying the irreversibility of Time. The moments he cherishes are those in which he successfully opposes the flow of Time by, for example, handling his mother's family momentos: "par delà les années, le temps supprimé, comme l'épiderme même des ambitions, des rêves, des vanités, des futiles et impérissables passions" (*RF*, 55). A successful reconstruction of a past life would become a duplicating process capable of negating man's destiny by negating that which makes him mortal: the steady, unwavering passage of Time.

The compulsion to "reflectively *re*possess"[14] an enduring image of self from the recesses of Time by delving into one's own past or the pasts of others, is also the central problem in *L'Herbe, Le Palace, Histoire* and *La Bataille de Pharsale*, which, together with *La Route des Flandres,* have often been termed the "memory novels." Elements which induce a pilgrimage backward into the past are noticeably more varied in *Histoire* (and in *L'Herbe* as well), since key items in the family house, encounters with a banker and antique dealer, and a café setting all provide the necessary stimulus for further retrospection. The one episode that generates a major portion of the narrator's temporal displacement is his examination of old post cards and family momentos belonging to his deceased mother. He refers to her post cards as "fragments, écailles arrachées à la surface de la vaste terre" (*HI,* 19). Like his own recurrent memories that are oftentimes disconnected from one another, the post cards represent isolated instances from his mother's life that no longer have any apparent structuring principle: "pêle-mêle dans le tiroir entassées sans ordre, les années se confondant s'intervertissant" (*HI,* 21). His task is to align, order, and finally make sense out of the many implications and potentially viable hypotheses surrounding each post card, much like the way he endeavors to read into his own past, always weighing the many possibilities: "traçant à l'encre mauve de son écriture haute épineuse rigide la réponse (mais quelle formule banale décente calmement passionnée?) qui parviendra trois semaines ou un mois plus tard dans quel désert quel marécage ou quel palace au luxe oriental et puritain" (*HI,* 31). And like Georges or O. in *La Bataille de Pharsale,* he too hopes to reveil the mystery that, legitimately or not, seems to encompass the figure of de Reixach. He wonders, for example, what de Reixach felt and what he thought about before he died.

A photo of Uncle Charles causes the narrator to speculate on his uncle's environment as an artist in Paris. Along with the multitude of photos, paintings, post cards, and sculptures that permeate Simon's fiction, this particular photo intrigues the narrator in *Histoire* because it draws his attention to the fascinating property of all photography, which is its fixed character in Time: "tandis que les autres personnes présentes, conservant pendant ces quelques secondes l'attitude qu'elles avaient au moment de l'ouverture de l'obturateur, semblent pour ainsi dire nier le temps, donnant l'illusion que la photographie est un de ces instantanés, une de ces coupes lamelliformes pratiquées à l'intérieur de la durée" (*HI,* 258-260). Like a lone image from years gone by, it exists in and of itself as an isolated work with no preface or post-script. The narrator's reaction is an immediate desire to know much more about the photo's past: "Plus tard seulement ils (les autres personnages figurant sur la photo) étaient venus occuper leurs places. Mais comment? Suivant quel ordre?" (*HI*, 271). The same is true of his repeated remembrances concerning certain war experiences or personal incidents with his father, mother, grandmother, cousin, and ex-wife. At base, the nephew, like Georges, O., and the student in *Le Palace,* adheres to the Proustain belief that the fullest possible understanding of the world and his relationship to it calls for a concentrated effort to rebuild and reintegrate himself with the past. As in modern psychoanalysis, Simon's narrators seek to return to those traumas or incidents which have never been successfully understood and which, because of their enigmatic qualities, attest to the fragmented nature of the self in Time.

In *La Bataille de Pharsale,* the narrator's mental odysseys into memories and fantasies of the past are chiefly stimulated by the physical objects located in front of him on his writing desk. A package of Gauloises cigarettes, for example, arouses the following war associations which relate to the narrator's own experiences on the battlefield and to his later efforts to situate the ancient battle of Pharsalus geographically on the plains of Thessaly: "Touchant presque le bas du dictionnaire et à demi dans son ombre se trouve un paquet de gauloises. Sur son enveloppe bleue est dessiné un casque pourvu d'ailes. Le casque fait penser à des bruits de métal entrechoqué, de batailles, à Vercingétorix, à des longues moustaches pendantes, à Jules César. Les ailes évoquent des images d'oiseaux, de plumes, de flèches empennées" (*BP*, 257). Although they are two very distinct points in Time, the battles at Pharsalus and on the Flandres Road are incidents to which he continuously refers and through which he compulsively re-interprets the past: "est-ce qu'il y avait vraiment un terrain de football comment aurait-il pu y en avoir au milieu de toute cette caillasse il faudrait vérifier mais vérifier quoi" (*BP*, 97). Likewise, the human, animal, and mechanical activity outside the narrator's apartment window also become the present tense phenomena that stir up thoughts of the past. In fact, O. begins his narrative with the image seen from his window of a bird in flight, an image that sets off a whole series of war-oriented memories and fantasies based on past experiences. Numerous other descriptions of present tense phenomena provide the impetus for recalling incidents in wartime, marriage, and adolescence. Certainly, the development of complex patterns of word associations becomes markedly more sophisticated in *La Bataille de Pharsale, Les Corps conducteurs, Triptyque,* and *Leçon de choses* than in earlier novels like *La Route des Flandres.* As Simon has said of his own most recent works: "chaque mot est porteur d'une charge à la fois historique, culturelle, phonétique. . .ce n'est pas non plus par hasard enfin que s'est *formé* ce vaste ensemble de *figures* métaphoriques dans et par quoi se dit le monde."[15]

In general, efforts toward an accurate recollection of the past in *La Bataille de Pharsale* focus on incidents involving wartime episodes in Spain and France, a train ride to Italy, an attempt to relocate the historical site of Caesar's battle at Pharsalus, childhood memories of Corinne and Uncle Charles, and the infidelity of an unidentified lover. O., like Georges and the nephew in *Histoire,* hopes to release himself from the destructive quality of a progressive, chronological Time by recovering a lost personal continuity and, in so doing, eternalize the self in a permanent order. This is the basic need behind each narrator's frantic yearning to "get at" the truth of a particularly perplexing memory such as de Reixach's murder-suicide:

> l'oeil immobile et attentif de son assassin patient l'index
> sur la détente voyant pour ainsi dire l'envers de ce que je
> pouvais voir ou moi l'envers et lui l'endroit c'est-à-dire
> qu'à nous deux moi le suivant et l'autre le regardant
> s'avancer nous possédions la totalité de l'énigme (l'assas-
> sin sachant ce qui allait lui arriver et moi sachant ce qui lui
> était arrivé, c'est-à-dire après et avant. . .) . . .il lui aurait
> fallu une glace à plusieurs faces, alors il aurait pu se voir
> lui-même. . . (*RF,* 313-314)

Georges realizes, however, that he would have had to be situated ahead of de Reixach; that is to say, ahead of death, as well as behind him in order to know whether or not de Reixach anticipated the assassin's bullets. To pierce through the ambiguities of that event and to perceive with accuracy the before and after surrounding it, or any other memory, would signify an escape from the irreversible flow of Time and a denial of the inherent subjectivity in all views of the past. Indeed, if such a liberation were possible, it would truly unite man with god.

Failures of Self-Reconstruction

Despite their aspirations for duration, each narrator's search for an object of faith hidden in memories and fantasies of distant events is thwarted again and again by the gap that always separates past from present. As Emily Zantz argues in her study of the novels of Butor, Robbe-Grillet, and Sarraute, closing the rift that invariably exists between man and the world would mean establishing a definite and fixed order to human experience— but such an order is never possible given the phenomenological assumptions of the *nouveau roman.*[16]   For if, in fact, man's *present* relationship to the world as well as his interpretations of those things that comprise it are constantly called into question, as they are in Simon's fiction, the past offers even less stability and clarity of perception because it is just that much more removed from man's immediate awareness. "Quels que soient les jeux de mots et les acrobaties de la logique," Camus has warned us, "comprendre c'est avant tout unifier."[17]   Simon's narrators would like to arrive at a definitive understanding of their own individuality in the world but are incapable of doing so by the very nature of consciousness itself, which is forever changing and modifying its status in, and perceptions of, the surrounding environment.

Thus, remembrance in Simon's fiction can never be an effectively cohesive act that integrates lost images of self since it so often emphasizes the distance existing between present time and remembered past. Embracing a rigorous philosophical framework, Minkowski defines the insurmountable abyss that severs past from present in the following terms:

> Remembrance puts us, in a direct way, in relation with a 'mediate' past. There is no remembrance for the present which just disappeared, no remembrance for a past losing itself in the infinite. Remembrance always bears on an event which happened "some time ago"; and however short this "some time ago" may be, it nonetheless constitutes *a lapse of time* from the qualitative point of view, *an open interval* during which the past even has not been

> present to consciousness in any way. Remembrance thus
> *juxtaposes,* in an immediate way and by itself, *two points
> of time,* in the form of the present and of a point of the
> past *separated* from each other by an empty interval with
> respect to the event in question. In other words, in ap-
> pearing to consciousness after an indeterminate interval,
> it tells us not only that an event of the past has been but,
> further, that it is no longer. And reason, which, like
> nature, has a *horror of a void,* is terrified in the presence
> of all of these givens full of contradiction and puts every-
> thing to work to suppress them.[18] (italics mine)

In short then, remembrance in the Simonian text calls our
attention to the "lapse of time" that juxtaposes a physical
present and a mental past. Understood in this way, each narra-
tor's attempt to reconstruct an enduring self from snapshot
memories of the past is an impossible, sisyphistic task: "c'est
partir du désaccord fondamental qui sépare l'homme de son
expérience pour trouver un terrain d'entente selon sa nostalgie,
un univers corsété de raisons ou éclairé d'analogies qui permette
de résoudre le divorce insupportable."[19]

　　In more concrete terms, the void that separates past from
present impedes each narrator's visual and auditory contact
with past events. For Georges, who attempts a mental recrea-
tion of the memories and fantasies that haunt him, it is as if he
were seeing through a heavy fog, hearing voices at a great dis-
tance: "ces quelques images muettes, à peine animées, vues de
loin" (*RF,* 50). While he may, in fact, remember the verbal
exchanges in a given conversation, he often has difficulty de-
termining who was speaking each line: "et Georges (ou Blum)
. . ." (*RF,* 188). At times, he confuses the speakers altogether.
Elsewhere, Georges resembles a frustrated contemporary movie-
goer watching an old silent film when the dialogue he tries to
reconstruct for the characters from his past remains entirely
inaudible: "Georges pouvant voir remuer leurs lèvres, mais
pas entendre (trop loin, caché derrière le temps, tandis qu'il
écoutait. . .)" (*RF,* 49). The narrator in *Histoire* encounters
similar difficulties, evoking images from past years that seem
to slip in and out of his consciousness like water: "(les dorures
les vieilles reines l'épouvantail fardé les peintures le portrait) se
dissociant se désagrégeant se dissolvant à toute vitesse s'estom-
pant s'effaçant absorbé bu comme par la trame de l'écran vide

grisâtre" (*HI*, 91). Thus conceived, the past is little more than a series of fugitive cinematographic scenes, shot from a great distance, flashing on and off the screen of our inner eye in rapid succession.

And just as the cinema presents the viewer with a limited perspective on one or more incidents from life as we know or imagine it, so too human memory provides the consciousness with a select group of images from the past that reflect the private, physical, and psychological make-up of a particular individual. In another instance, for example, the narrator in *Histoire* likens the memory process to a blurred black and white photo that renders certain peripheral forms unclear: "l'amincissement des formes à demi mangées en même temps que le flou de la mauvaise mise au point achève de donner au tout cet aspect un peu fantomatique des dessins exécutés au fusain et à l'estompe et où les contours ne sont pas délimités par un trait mais où les volumes apparaissent saillant hors de l'ombre ou s'y enfonçant tour à tour comme dans la mémoire" (*HI*, 283). The photo of Uncle Charles in this ninth section of *Histoire* is the object of the narrator's careful study while he tries to conceptualize Charles' presumably arty life in Paris. However, after formulating and rejecting numerous hypotheses, he finally acknowledges that the blurred areas of the photo are as indefinite and unintelligible as those aspects of Charles' past that the nephew has also failed to piece together in a coherent fashion. For the task of mirroring the pasts of others is even more vain than the effort to mirror one's own history. Hence the failure of the camera eye is analogous to the internal failure of human memory: both processes are unable to lighten as well as give form and meaning to those obscure contours that surround any event from our pasts or those of others.

Despite their fervent desire to anchor an image of self in their past experiences, at some point all of Simon's narrators must come to terms with the failure of human consciousness to mirror even present exterior reality both exactly and completely. Needless to say, mirroring the past, which is an external world even more remote from man's consciousness, becomes an exercise in futility. Often incapable of distinguishing external facts from internal fantasies or personal opinions, the narrative consciousness is often caught in the cross-fire, vacillating from one point-of-view to another in an attempt at exactitude. In one instance, for example, Georges is admittedly confused as to the *real* existence of Corinne's red dress since he may have invented it when thinking of her lips or her name, Corinne, which he associates with coral. And he is no more certain about the nature of de Reixach's death: was he unexpectedly murdered by the enemy or did he realize the trap and choose it as a noble suicide gesture? And if it was indeed suicide, what were the motives behind the act? His wife's infidelity? The humiliating loss of his regiment at the hands of the enemy? To these questions and to others, Georges' responses are, at best, tentative. Even his language echoes the confusion of consciousness amid embroidered fantasy and potential fact: "peut-être," "probablement," "sinon pourquoi," "sans doute," and most significant of all, "mais encore une fois comment le savoir. . ." (*RF*, 214). These unending questions cause the narrative consciousness such hesitancy that it is forever conjecturing on the possible or probable, struggling to patch disparate elements together only to disassemble them at some further point in time with the introduction of a new hypothesis. Past events contend with one another in the narrator's mind to such an extent that, as Robbe-Grillet notes of Beckett's trilogy, "la même phrase peut contentir une constatation et sa négation immédiate."[20]

When asked about the reasons behind his earlier participation in the Spanish Civil War, the nephew-narrator in *Histoire* responds that he no longer knows why he went there nor what he had hoped to accomplish. Moreover, he too questions the accuracy of his recollections when, at one point, he envisions the family members gathered around his dying mother: "comme s'ils étaient tous venus là se réunir pour la regarder mourir, assis maintenant autour d'elle immobiles figés dans des poses méditatives et. . .Mais exactement?" (*HI*, 78). Similarly, the narrator in *La Bataille de Pharsale* remembers the hardships incurred during his stay in Greece when he endeavored to map out the ancient battle site of Pharsalus. There was more wisdom than he had at first realized in the old Greek's response to his inquiries: "Avant le Christ Mais alors comment savoir?" (*BP*, 30). Repeatedly, the exterior world of the past and the interior world of consciousness clash in Simon's novels, causing a discontinuity of self in Time. Reminiscent once more of Proust's Marcel, the narrative consciousness is "unable to live fully in the instant and unable, save at crucial turnings, to recover the instant in its uniqueness."[21]

There is, in addition, another kind of temporal distortion occurring in Simon's fiction that stems from the narrator's own confusion of individuals as well as incidents. As readers, we discover that the conventional boundaries which normally delineate self from other, or ancestor from friend, progressively break-down in each novel. In *La Route des Flandres,* Georges shifts at times from a fantasy about his long-deceased ancestor in the family portrait to a remembered description of Captain de Reixach without even acknowledging any distinction between the two men. Likewise, the nephew in *Histoire* often has considerable difficulty untangling Charles' life from his own. The interchangeability of characters develops to such an extent that ultimately, in *La Bataille de Pharsale,* both narrator and reader are unable to distinguish Uncle Charles, his mistress, the narrator, and his lover from one another since they are all four referred to alternately as "O." Jean Ricardou has speculated that the very use of the letter O. to represent a number of different characters may be significant: "cette lettre circulaire que nous lisons O peut aussi bien s'entendre comme ce chiffre circulaire qu'il faut lire zéro, et par lequel l'amenuisement du personnage serait signalé comme très proche de son terme."[22]

In any event, it seems clear that with the growing interchange of roles and the obscuring of normal personality traits, Simon's narrators can no longer lean on the stability of others, events, or even themselves in History because all of these elements are no more than visions, dreams, or nightmares of a self forever groping in the semi-darkness of the past. Everything, including a past image of self, is subject to change since each narrator's interpretations of History depend upon his present state of mind, which is always being transformed by the changing phenomena that surround him. Indeed, the past literally becomes a *present* memory experience of a thing already removed from us.[23] Because it always remains subordinate to our present orientation in the world, the past can never be concretely reconstructed. John Sturrock has argued even more generally that "the New Novel subscribes to the old Platonic belief that imagination is memory, and what it does is to dramatize the processes of imagination. This involves a partial, or in some cases, a total disconnection of the mind from the events of the external world."[24] This is to a large degree true in Simon's fiction and furthermore it explains why, for example, the narrator in *Histoire* falls short of solidifying images of the past in his mind: "ils seront là s'agitant

parlant tous à la fois avec leurs orbites vides. . .puis ils sombre-
ront de nouveau s'enfonceront continuant encore un moment à
gesticuler comme les passagers d'un navire lentement submergé
disparaissant peu à peu dans les épaisseurs du temps et moi
impuissant les regardant s'engloutir lentement s'effacer con-
servant l'image d'un dernier visage d'une dernière bouche" (*HI,*
395). He is powerless over not only the accuracy but also the
duration of these fleeting pictures from the past since his own
identity in Time and in the world is ambiguous and in a constant
state of alteration.

The non-linear quality of the past as it is evoked or re-
experienced in the *lived present* is yet another factor attesting to
the discontinuous nature of Time in Simon's fiction.[25] In the
final analysis, his narrators are always unsuccessful at erecting an
objective chronology or series of casual relationships between
various events occurring in distant points of Time. As Minkowski
has observed, the past always seems to be severed from the lived
present because it is characterized by the existence of disparate
historical data which are at base devoid of meaning, lacking a
connection between them, and ultimately destined to oblivion:

> The passage of the past into the present does not
> have a linear character. Try as I may to represent facts
> or events to myself and to establish a connection between
> them, either in the form of causality or in the more
> vibrant form of evolution or progress, and try as I may to
> breathe new life into these facts and to make them live
> again before me, it remains that only isolated facts will be
> related in this way, and the present, understood as the
> lived present, cannot thereby be deduced in any man-
> ner.[26]

It is the indisputably fragmented nature of the past that defies
each narrator's efforts to reorder and decipher it. And as a re-
sult, O.'s compulsive need to "reprendre, ordonner, Première-
ment, deuxièmement, troisièmement" (*BP,* 184) must finally
fail. Like the nephew in *Histoire,* he too recognizes the evanes-
cent quality of those mental images emanating from the past:
"tout retombant, après l'assourdissant tapage des bétonneuses
et des ordres criés, dans le silence originel dont la terre et la mer
n'ont sans doute été tirées que pour qu'existe quelque part,
inutile, . . .un endroit où les navires puissent venir mourir les

uns après les autres" (*HI*, 58). After numerous abortive attempts at stabilizing a clear relationship between present self and past events, the narrators relinquish all previous belief pertaining to the linear, progressive nature of History.

In *La Route des Flandres,* Georges chides his father, Pierre, for his insistent belief in cultural progress, despite all the blatant evidence to the contrary during World War II. In a letter to his son, Pierre laments the bombing of the famous Leipzig library and predicts that History will criticize such a blasphemous annihilation of the highly organized, bound heritage of several centuries. But Georges merely retorts: "si le contenu des milliers de bouquins de cette irremplaçable bibliothèque avait été précisément impuissant à empêcher que se produisent des choses comme le bombardement qui l'a détruite, je ne voyais pas très bien quelle perte représentait pour l'humanité la disparition sous les bombes au phosphore de ces milliers de bouquins et de papelards manifestement dépourvus de la moindre utilité" (*RF*, 224). Georges' cynical response carries with it two messages: first, it reflects a deep-seated mistrust of words and their inability to improve the human condition, and second, it indicates his acute sensitivity to the dubious role of reason in human history. C.-G. Bjurstrom has, it seems, accurately described Simon's repudiation of History in its traditionally western profile when he concludes that "Simon rejette comme une abstraction insupportable l'Histoire avec un H, à la fois sous sa forme traditionnaliste et sous son aspect marxiste: la prétention de pouvoir donner aux évènements un lien, une suite conséquente, une évolution et finalement une valeur, ne lui paraît être qu'un méprisable alibi moral."[27]

Because the past is never experienced as anything more than a series of isolated images having little or no causal relationship to one another, the interrogations of a self searching for identity amid its past continue to go unanswered. For although the self may indeed equal the sum of its past experiences, the historical past always eludes definition in Simon's fiction, revealing only distinctly separate moments the significance of which remain undecipherable. It is for this reason that the pictoral images in the minds of his narrators cannot serve as a vehicle for the recupersation of the past, as they did in Proust's masterpiece, since they do not retrieve a particular retrospective existence. On the contrary, they tend to accentuate, even highlight the continual vacillation and turmoil of a human consciousness unsure of its personal roots in the past and equally perplexed about its grounding in the present. By extension, then, we may deduce that for Simon the artistic process or narrative journey can never lead to the successful recovery of a self lost in the confusion of the past. As Simon himself has commented, "Il me semble que l'on ne sauve jamais rien de ce qui est perdu. . .La recherche de Proust ne l'a pas conduit à retrouver le temps, mais à produire un objet écrit qui a sa propre temporalité. Je crois que pas plus qu'il ne peut être témoignage (sauf indirectement et pas par ce qui le constitue en tant qu'art), l'art ne peut être non plus une entreprise de récupération."[28] Hence the narrative quest for an individuated life lost in Time progressively loses ground in Simon's fiction as his narrators become increasingly alert to the futility of their obsessive pursuit. Like History itself, human duration is most often experienced as a plethora of separate, hazy images, each one contesting the other, leaving man assured only of his own ambiguity in Time and in the world. Certainly, the frontispiece in *Histoire* carries with it this fundamental meaning:

> Cela nous submerge.   Nous l'organisons.   Cela
> tombe en morceaux.
> Nous l'organisons de nouveau et tombons
> nous-mêmes en morceaux.
> Rilke (*HI*, 7)

Toward a Temporal Transcendence

It seems, then, that Simon's narrators have no firm hold on History, whether it be the history of a civilization, another individual, or even their own. In spite of their wish to discriminate among past experiences for the purposes of formulating a network of interconnected relationships contingent upon the forces of cause and effect, they all come to realize that memories and particular viewpoints are selected altogether arbitrarily: "peut-être as-tu raison après tout tout savoir ne débouche jamais que sur un autre savoir et les mots sur d'autres mots" (*BP*, 18). Even those events recorded in the most rigid empirical style must be subject to suspicion. Such is the case, for example, in *La Bataille de Pharsale* when the narrator questions Caesar's description of the ancient battle at Thessaly: "Rien d'autre que quelques mots quelques signes sans consistance matérielle comme tracés sur de l'air assemblés conservés recopiés traversant les couches incolores du temps des siècles à une vitesse foudroyante remontant des profondeurs et venant crever à la surface comme des bulles vides comme des bulles et rien d'autre Clair pour qui ne cherche pas à l'approfondir" (*BP*, 91). Historical truth or objectivity is never more than provisional, at best, since Simon's narrators experience both past and present as part of an apparently continual flux of sensuous impressions and snap-shot images.

The very notion of History as a systematic recording, analysis, and rational explanation of past events seems to be severely undermined in Simon's fiction. This is not surprising, however, when we consider that the ability to know as well as to account for anything that has happened in the past requires a constancy in the analyst's point-of-view that Simon's narrators, like Sartre's Roquentin or Beckett's Molloy, fail to duplicate due to their own internal confusion and flux. Indeed, for these narrators, the past continually eludes them, appearing only as a discontinuous series of fleeting photographic images that are most often perceived as distinctly out of focus. For this reason, disciplined attempts to chart historical chronology and causality are presented as fool-hardy ventures that the narrators ridicule more and more as their narratives progress: "l'histoire (ou si tu préfères: la sottise, le courage, l'orgueil, la souffrance) ne laisse derrière elle qu'un résidu abusivement confisqué, désinfecte et enfin comestible, à l'usage des manuels scolaires agréés et des familles à pédigree" (*RF*, 188). A rational approach to History demands that the consciousness organize all of the various aspects of life into a coherent system of interrelated parts communicated through formal language channels. Yet such a mode of cognition can only reduce the complexity of existence by eliminating its ambiguities and its mysteries. Gusdorf concurs when he writes that "il semble bien que la raison soit née comme la conscience de la science. Elle s'efforce de déterminer les faits et les notions en les séparant, en les spécifiant, en les réduisant. Connaissance, ici, signifie désintégration. . .Le signe de la raison est la transparence, la réductibilité."[29] In Simon's novels, the theoretical exercise of separating people and events into pragmatic categories for discursive and deductive purposes is viewed, finally, as a reductive process rather than as an exploratory inquiry into the irrational and contradictory elements in life.

It is true that much of what the narrators review in their pasts and in Western History emphasizes the chaotic, irrational forces at work in the cosmos. Serge Doubrovsky has gone so far as to argue that disorder is the thematic focus in all of Simon's fiction.[30] If, however, discernable patterns can be found in the passage of individual, social, and cosmological Time, they must lie in the *repetitive* forms that run throughout History. This is, in effect, the historical posture that has been alluded to in the three preceding sections wherein we have traced the emergence of a number of key archetypal configurations apparent in but not restricted to *La Route des Flandres, Histoire,* and *La Bataille de Pharsale.* This repetitive perception of History speaks to the issues of equivocation, ambiguity, and contradiction in ways that platonism, cartesianism, or rationalism, would never have deemed acceptable. In addition, the concept of repetition negates to a large degree the theory of human perfectability and universal progress. Primarily influenced by Jung and Bachelard, Gilbert Durand considers this historical mode of cognition as it relates to what he terms "le régime nocturne de l'image:" "Face aux visages du temps une autre attitude imaginative se dessine donc, consistant à capter les forces vitales du devenir, à exorciser les idoles meurtrières de Kronos, à les transmuter en talismans bénéfiques, enfin à incorporer à l'inéluctable mouvance du temps les rassurantes figures de constantes, de cycles qui au sein même du devenir semblent accomplir un dessein éternel."[31] Hence while historical repetition denies progression, it also calls our attention to those *ritual* acts or events that appear as stable points of reference in the great flux of life, past and present.

According to Stanley Hyman and numerous other myth critics, a ritual is "the anonymous regular recurrence of an action," whereas the historical event is that which occurs only once, "the unique identifiable experience in time."[32] And so it is that the confused repetitions and perplexing circularity of events in Simon's fiction gain a new significance as ritualistic activities that reinscribe order in the universe. For man in an archaic society, every ritual has an archetype or model who performed the act for the first time *in illo tempore,* that is, in the mythic beginnings.[33]   For Simon's narrators, however, the archetypes do not necessarily emerge from the beginnings of Time, but often from the beginnings of Western civilization—such is the case, for example, with the narrators' extensive use of classical and biblical mythology, which establishes imitable patterns inherent in archetypal figures and situations.   Thus, the role of ritual is to provide a perennial form for human life and to project the individual out of his or her particular identity, into a universal mold.   It is apparently within this frame of reference that Georges singles out the prominent characteristics in his companions during the war: "peut-être ces choses je veux dire l'intelligence l'idiotie ou être amoureux ou brave ou lâche ou meurtrier les qualités les passions existent-elles en dehors de nous venant se loger sans nous demander notre avis dans cette grossière carcasse qu'elles possèdent" (*RF*, 118).   The verb "posséder" is an interesting one when used in this context because it stresses how little control man has over his own particular reactions and how much he is governed by enduring human feelings and drives.   Whether we attribute these recurrent patterns to what many have termed the "unconscious" or simply refer to them as exterior forces whose place of origin is unknown, as Georges does, the end result is the same.   In both instances, the divestiture of uniquely personal characteristics is a paradoxical transformation, for, as Eliade has noted, the individual actually becomes himself, that is to say, his *essential* self, when he ceases to be a particular being in order to imitate an archetype.[34]

Whether or not it is firmly couched in a specific historical period and/or spatial locale, the archetype performing the ritual alerts us to the symbolic structures of being in the world. Moreover, both the blatantly ceremonial and the more mundane, compulsive acts may give rise to archetypal patterns of behavior. While the nephew-narrator in *Histoire* recalls even the most minute details of the old ladies who visited his home during his youth, the image we are left with is a depersonalized one in which the aging women and their old Germanic predecessors are fused together due to their perpetually mysterious aloofness, even in the face of physical disintegration:

> . . .cette aura d'obscure puissance qui les entourait toutes: vaguement fantastiques, vaguement incrédibles, retirées dans leur royale solitude, cette roide majesté qui contrastait avec leur fragilité physique, et ce privilège exclusif

qu'elles détenaient, puisqu'on disait d'elles qu'elles
allaient bientôt mourir, tout—jusqu'à ces maquillages
maladroits—concourant à leur conférer l'aspect mythique
et fabuleux d'êtres à mi-chemin entre l'humain, l'animal
et le surnaturel, siégeant comme ces aréopages de
créatures (juges ou divinités souterraines) qui detiennent
la clef d'un monde paré du prestige de l'inaccessible (*HI*,
13)

The lack of individual names, a technique employed by modern
writers like Proust, Robbe-Grillet, and Nathalie Sarraute, or the
repetition of names and surnames, as in Faulkner's fiction or
Ionesco's theatre, coupled with commonly shared human ideals,
experiences, and obsessions work to instill each of Simon's
novels with recurrent models of human action as well as a for-
midable sense of *déjà vu*.   J. A. E. Loubère has also suggested
that with the stripping away or "denuding," as she terms it, of
the human character in *Les Corps conducteurs*, Simon is able to
emphasize even more insistently the universal rather than the
distinctly personal qualities of human experience.[35]

From a functional perspective, myths, archetypes, and
symbolic modes of human activity are intimately related, al-
though not necessarily synonymous, in that they all furnish the
human spirit with permanent designs in daily reality capable of
transcending the limited boundaries of a highly personalized
image of life. One such example, as has previously been sug-
gested, is the potentially confining image of the Flanders Road
that moves beyond its particular socio-historic setting by virtue
of the continual associations to still other wartime defeats. In
this way, one spatially situated event is simultaneously viewed
in a myriad of other spatial locations, creating an endless *mise en
abyme* out of what we would normally consider to be rationally
distinct, juxtaposed points in Time and Space. Michel Leiris
has already recognized the implications of this same universaliz-
ing technique in Michel Butor's *La Modification* and he has
appropriately termed it "le réalisme mythologique."[36]

The basic principle linking rite and archetype to mythology
and, on a broader scale, to mythic awareness is the perennial and
exemplary nature of the patterns they reveal through human
action. Mythology, Campbell assures us, "places our true being
not in the forms that shatter but in the imperishable out of

which they again immediately bubble forth. . ."[37] And because rites, archetypes, and mythological motifs point to the repetitive human practices and emotional states, they become vehicles capable of suppressing the passage of Time. In essence, mythic awareness stabilizes temporal discontinuity by bridging the void between past and present. This is what accounts for O.'s fascination with the Roman marble freeze in *La Bataille de Pharsale*, which somehow captures the recurrent odyssey of men on horseback riding to their deaths: "les vagues silhouettes galopantes aux entrailles de pierre semblent s'enfoncer dans les entrailles grisâtres et compliquées de la pierre, du temps, où l'écho silencieux de leur galop, l'éclat, parfois du soleil sur les mèches d'une crinière, un hennissement, la trace minérale de leurs ombres, rappellent qu'ils continuent leur course" (*BP*, 265). Most of the paintings, frescoes, freezes, and literary works referred to in Simon's novels seem to generate this transcendent quality and, in so doing, manage to establish a new realism that is neither subjective nor objective, but *mythic*.

The conceivably tragic implications of wars, approaching death, political disasters, and scarred inter-personal relationships are invariably softened or even negated altogether when set within a mythic perspective. For myth is eminently *un*tragical because the beginning anew of the same behavior pattern is implicit in its ending.[38] This mythic mode of cognition accounts for much of the cynicism of Simon's narrators. They mock those who would believe themselves capable of implementing radical and permanent changes such as those ambitious leaders like Caesar or Hitler, the devoted Left in the Spanish Civil War with their cry to arms: "VENCEREMOS," the French political posters heralding a "UNION POUR LE PROGRES," or the allegorical victory painting in *La Route des Flandres:* "les successives générations d'électeurs écoutant discourir les successives générations de politiciens auxquels cette victoire avait conféré le droit de discourir—et aux auditeurs celui de les écouter discourir—sur l'estrade drapée de tricolore" (*RF*, 215). It is because of the cyclic nature of human and natural events, regardless of our conscious endeavors to avert them, that Simon's narrators regard all such aspirations for progress from a cynical stance.

The mythic perspective actually domesticates Time by refuting the significance of its passing. And, to be sure, the

extensive use of the present participle in *La Route des Flandres*,
Le Palace, and *Histoire* is an ingenious literary device for enabling
Simon's narrators to stress, whether consciously or unconscious-
ly, duration and constancy across a variety of spatio-temporal
spheres.[39]   In this sense, using the present participle manipulates
Time by eliminating its traditionally rational, scientific categories
in order to accentuate the *eternally present* qualities inherent in
mythic awareness.   The final passage in *La Route des Flandres*
clearly exemplifies this technique as the narrator turns his
thoughts to a previous war experience and slowly becomes en-
gulfed by it.   This psychological progression is distinctly mirrored
in his more and more frequent use of the present participle and
the simple present which enables him and the reader to transcend
the temporal boundaries of past and present:

> Mais l'ai-je vraiment vu ou cru le voir ou tout simplement
> imaginé après coup ou encore rêvé, peut-être dormais-je
> n'avais-je jamais cessé de dormir les yeux grands ouverts
> en plein jour bercé par le martèlement monotone des
> sabots des cinq chevaux *piétinant* leurs ombres ne *mar-
> chant* pas exactement à la même cadence de sorte que
> c'était comme un crépitement *alternant se rattrapant se
> superposant se confondant* par moments comme s'il n'y
> avait plus qu'un seul cheval, puis *se dissociant* de nouveau
> *se désagrégeant recommençant* semblait-il à se courir
> après et cela ainsi de suite, la guerre pour ainsi dire *étale*
> pour ainsi dire paisible autour de nous, le canon spor-
> adique *frappant* dans les vergers déserts avec un bruit
> sourd monumental et creux comme une porte en train de
> battre agitée par le vent dans une maison vide, le paysage
> tout entier inhabité vide sous le ciel immobile, le monde
> arrêté figé *s'effritant se dépiautant s'écroulant* peu à peu
> par morceaux comme une bâtisse abandonnée, inutili-
> sable, livrée à l'incohérent, nonchalant, impersonnel et
> destructeur travail du temps. (*RF,* 314, italics mine)

The narrative technique for transcending temporal divisions
is even more direct in *La Bataille de Pharsale.* Here, the narrator
relies almost entirely on the simple present and the present
participle verb forms in his descriptions. When not using these
forms, he has a tendency to avoid verbs altogether, employing
nouns to describe activity as he does in the beginning of the
novel:

Jaune et puis noir temps d'un *battement* de pau-
pières et puis jaune de nouveau: ailes déployées forme
d'arbalète rapide entre le soleil et l'oeil *ténèbres un
instant* sur le visage comme un velours une main un
instant *ténèbres* puis *lumière* ou plutôt *emémoration
(avertissement?) rappel* des ténèbres *jaillissant* de bas en
haut à une foudroyante *rapidité* plapables c'est-à-dire
successivement le menton la bouche le nez le front *pou-
vant* les *sentir* et même olfactivement leur odeur moisie
de caveau de tombeau comme une poignée de terre
noire *entendant* en même temps le bruit de soie déchirée
. . . (*BP,* 9, italics mine)

So it seems that in the face of the apparent chaos of per-
sonal, social, and historical events, there exists a homogeneous
consistency capable of fusing two or more distant beings or
occurrences into a dynamic association freed from the confines
of Time and Space. Personal anxieties and historical biases are
thereby superseded in Simon's fiction by those primordial images
of man which lie buried in each narrator's mythological and
archetypal symbolisms: the result being that duration is super-
imposed upon a persistantly fluctuating universe. And with the
discovery of certain enduring qualities, the world is again en-
dowed with an order that attempts to reintegrate man into the
universal rhythms: "le mythe a pour fonction de rendre la vie
possible. Il donne aux sociétés humaines leur assiette et leur
permet de durer."[40]

Although Simon's narrators fail in their attempts to verify
historical data or recapture a personal identity through mental
reconstructions of details lost in Time, they manage nevertheless
to retrieve a number of transtemporal human expressions that
release the self from a progressive, chronological order by form-
ing a sense of continuity with the universal man. The narrative
consciousness and the reader, who partakes in the intimate
ramblings of a human mind, experience being in the world as
both temporal and atemporal. The temporal exerts its influence
through the inevitable passage of Time, the movement of all life
toward death, and the enormous difficulty of objectively reliving
events in a given past, while the atemporal realm affirms its sig-
nificance through the continual reappearance of mythological
and archetypal figures and settings that refuse insertion in any
particular moment or place in History.

NOTES

[1]Carl Jung, "The Symbolic Life," a lecture given in 1939 and printed for private circulation only. Consult Erich Neumann's *The Origins and History of Consciousness*, trans. by R. F. C. Hull (1949; rpt. Princeton: Princeton University Press, 1954), pp. 369-370.

[2]Mircea Eliade, *Myths, Dreams, and Mysteries*, trans. by Philip Mairet (1957; rpt. New York: Harper and Row, 1960), p. 34.

[3]Jean-René Huguenin, *Une Autre Jeunesse* (Paris: Seuil, 1965), p. 11.

[4]Consult Section I of this study for an earlier discussion of Leonardo's quotation.

[5]Eugène Minkowski, *Lived Time*, trans. by Nancy Metzel (1933; rpt. Evanston: Northwestern University Press, 1970), p. 134.

[6]Alan Harrington, *The Immortalist* (New York: Avon, 1969), pp. 107-108. Harrington argues that there are essentially four ways in which man avoids death: "1) the way of *standing out* against the laws of creation and decay. . . 2) the way of *retracting the self.* . . 3) the way of *deliberately dulling one's awareness of things.* . .and 4) the way of trying to by-pass death through the *gentle diffusion* or *violent shattering of the self.*"

[7]Brown, pp. 108-109.

[8]Minkowski, p. 132.

[9]Albert Camus, *Noces suivi de L'Eté* (Paris: Gallimard, 1959), p. 122.

[10]For further discussions of psychoanalysis as it relates to History, consult the following authors and their works: Mircea Eliade, *Myth and Reality* (New York: Harper and Row, 1963), Hans Meyerhoff, *Time in*

Literature (Berkeley: University of California Press, 1968), and Norman O. Brown, *Life Against Death.*

[11]Marcel Proust, *A la recherche du temps perdu* (Paris: La Pléiade, 1954), II, p. 351.

[12]Gilbert Durand, *Les Structures anthropologiques de l'imaginaire* (Paris: Bordas, 1969), p. 466.

[13]Several critics have studied Simon's use of the present participle. See, for example, Ludovic Janvier, *Une Parole exigeante* (Paris: Minuit, 1964) and John Sturrock, *The French New Novel.*

[14]Robert Champigny, "Proust, Bergson and Other Philosophers," in *Proust: A Collection of Critical Essays,* ed. by René Girard (Englewood Cliffs, New Jersey: Prentice-Hall, 1962), p. 124. Champigny uses the term "reflective possession" to describe Proust's impulse to write "in order to discover and recover: reflective possession, not constructive action, is the ultimate purpose."

[15]Claude Simon, "La Fiction mot à mot," in *Nouveau Roman: hier, aujourd'hui,* ed. by J. Ricardou and F. Van Rossum-Guyon (Paris: UGE, 1972), II, pp. 41-82.

[16]Emily Zantz, *The Aesthetics of the New Novel in France* (Boulder: University of Colorado Press, 1968).

[17]Albert Camus, *Le Mythe de Sisyphe* (Paris: Gallimard, 1942), p. 32.

[18]Minkowski, p. 168.

[19]Camus, *Le Mythe de Sisyphe,* p. 134.

[20]Alain Robbe-Grillet, *Pour un nouveau roman* (Paris: Minuit, 1963), p. 38.

[21]Richard Macksey, "The Architecture of Time: Dialectics and Structure" in *Proust: A Collection of Critical Essays,* p. 119.

[22]Jean Ricardou, "Le Nouveau Roman existe-t-il?" in *Nouveau Roman: hier, aujourd'hui,* I, p. 17.

[23]Meyerhoff, p. 8.

[24]Sturrock, p. 19.

[25]The *lived present* is a partial mode of temporal narration which Minkowski describes as "an account of the act that we execute while we are in the process of acting. . . ," p. 33.

[26]Minkowski, p. 165.

[27]C.-G. Bjurstrom, "Dimensions du temps chez Claude Simon" in *Entretiens: Claude Simon,* ed. by Marcel Séguier (Toulouse: Subervie, 1972), p. 151.

[28]Claude Simon, "Réponses de Claude Simon à quelques questions écrites de Ludovic Janvier" in *Entretiens: Claude Simon,* pp. 24-25.

[29]Georges Gusdorf, *Mythe et métaphysique* (Paris: Flammarion, 1953), p. 220.

[30]Doubrovsky argues that "la situation de base, le dilemme fonda- mental, chez Simon, sont posés bien avant *La Route:* concilier, articuler un *ordre* et un *désordre,* le désordre, irrémédiable du vécu et l'ordre arti- ficiel du langage. D'où la difficulté intrinsèque de la 'tentative de restitu- tion.' " See Serge Doubrovsky, "Notes sur la genèse d'une écriture," in *Entretiens: Claude Simon,* p. 52.

[31]Durand, p. 219.

[32]Stanley Edgar Hyman, "The Ritual View of Myth and the Mythic" in *Myth: A Symposium,* ed. by Thomas A. Sebeok (Bloomington: Indiana University Press, 1971), p. 146.

[33]See Mircea Eliade's *Cosmos and History,* trans. by Willard R. Trask (1949; rpt. New York: Harper and Row, 1959).

[34]*Ibid.,* p. 35.

[35]J. A. E. Loubère, *The Novels of Claude Simon* (Ithaca: Cornell University Press, 1975), p. 186.

[36]Michel Leiris, "Le Réalisme mythologique de Michel Butor" in Michel Butor's *La Modification* (Paris: UGE, 1957).

[37]Joseph Campbell, *The Hero with a Thousand Faces* (1949; rpt. New York: World, 1956), p. 269.

[38]*Ibid.*, pp. 269-270.

[39]Brian Fitch mentions the stabilizing effect of the present participle and adds that "le participe présent évoque un mouvement dont la durée n'est pas indiquée. . .nous ne voyons pas la naissance ni la mort d'un geste puisqu'il est déjà en cours." See Brian T. Fitch, "Participe présent et procédés narratifs chez Claude Simon" in *Un Nouveau Roman*, ed. by J. H. Matthews (Paris: Minard, 1964), pp. 200-201.

[40]Gusdorf, p. 19.

CONCLUSION

Simon's work in many ways exemplifies the radical changes initiated in the structure of consciousness by other practitioners of the *nouveau roman*. Like Samuel Beckett, Michel Butor, Alain Robbe-Grillet, and Nathalie Sarraute, Claude Simon continues to advocate the abstraction and, in some cases, virtual disappearance of the characters and narrators who once confidently populated the traditional novel. The multiplication of narrative perspectives is another technique that further challenges the reader of the new fiction by forcing him to acknowledge the relative subjectivity of all points of view and the consequent enigmatic quality of our world. As a prototype of the *nouveau roman*, Simon's mature fiction also reflects a new understanding of the creative process and of the human mind as well, which is based on the generating properties[1] of individual words, rather than on an over-all fictional scheme mapped-out in advance by the author. Simon himself calls this technique "la fiction mot à mot,"[2] suggesting the importance given to the associative power of each word in the creative act and in consciousness itself.

From the viewpoint of structure, Simon's novels since *Le Vent* adhere to the conspicuously non-linear form of the *nouveau* roman by continually returning to the same subject matter throughout the narrative. Recent novels such as *Les Corps conducteurs* and *Triptyque* further attest to Simon's creative interest in circularity and repetition. The composition of *Triptyque*, the author tells us, is inspired by three incidents, or stories, which "s'y entrelacent, se superposent parfois, se nourrissent l'une de l'autre et, finalement, s'effacent. . ."[3] Hence, contrary to what a cursory glance might first suggest, Simon's fiction, like that of other so-called "new novelists," is ordered to emphasize the cyclical, repetitive nature of the mind and of life itself. Experiential episodes that are repeated in expanded or contracted form have become a veritable commonplace in the Simonian text. In the end, the narratives often refer back to the initial imagery or situations of the opening sections, reminding us of Beckett's pithy assertion in *Endgame* that "the end is in the beginning and yet you go on." Unquestionably, Simon is deeply embedded in and committed to maintaining the dynamic revolutionary qualities that have given the *nouveau roman* its distinguishable character.

What seems certain, however, is that Simon's obvious alignment with this new tradition constitutes but one aspect of his fictional expression. In the final analysis, Simon's work is distinctive in the most profound sense of the word since it manages to conjoin both private and historical mythologies in a desire to delineate the properties that unify people, places, and things, past and present. As we have noted, looking backward at History readily becomes a meditation on the ever-recurring modes of human expression and behavior as they appear in mythological and archetypal imagery. History is thereby understood as a cyclic process, mirroring the natural birth, evolution, death, and dissolution of a single living being that ultimately contributes to the regeneration of other life forms in the organic world. Likewise, human societies and their substantive activities are born, decay, and perish only to be born anew at some later place in Time. As we have seen, this is particularly the case in *L'Herbe, La Route des Flandres, La Palace, Histoire, La Bataille de Pharsale,* as well as in his more recent fiction, where Simon treats war, revolution, imprisonment, and dictatorship as activities that occur so frequently as to seem expectable and ever-present in the natural pattern of the victory, decline, and fall of all sociopolitical institutions: "Je pouvais entendre de nouveau ce bruit [de guerre], ce bouillonnement, écoutant se séparer ce que l'été, la terre, le soleil, les pluies avaient peu à peu amalgamé et que la petite flamme silencieuse était en train de décomposer de nouveau, comme si tout ne faisait que se réunir, se combiner, se désunir de nouveau, comme si cela ne cessait jamais" (*HI*, 153). Throughout his literary texts we find that mythic awareness and a cyclical interpretation of History are commonly aligned in this fashion since both perspectives emphasize the repetitive nature of human events while undermining man's all too cherished belief in the ability of reason to apprehend and conceivably control reality.

The proliferation of mythological and archetypal imagery in Simon's major novels manages to construct a tone as well as a poetic framework through which the human mind reestablishes an equilibrium both in and with the world. And it is likely that this implicit transtemporal dimension accounts in part for the appeal of Simon's work, which otherwise verges at times on the hermetic. As our leading myth critics continually remind us, the goal of the mythic vision is analogous to that of the ancient mythologies, which strive to dispel human fear and ignorance by providing "a reconciliation of the individual consciousness with the universal will. And this is effected through a realization of the true relationship of the passing phenomena of time to the imperishable life that lives and dies in all."[4] If there are actual moments of epiphany in Simon's novels, they occur at such instances when the power of a recurrent image, like the ancient myths of the archaic world, enables a narrator limited in Space, Time, and Duration to discern his relationship to some of the more cohesive patterns of life and, as a result, allows him to move closer to the discovery of an essential human self embedded in the exemplary models of mythic consciousness. What is in question, then, in Simon's fiction is a modern narrative consciousness turned inward upon itself, evoking certain archetypes and mythological motifs in an attempt to decipher the secret, unknown symbolisms that fill its world.

NOTES

[1]Jean Ricardou has discussed the principle of generating words as it applies to Simon's *La Bataille de Pharsale* in his essay on "La bataille de la phrase," in *Pour une théorie du nouveau roman* (Paris: Seuil, 1971).

[2]See Claude Simon's article on "La fiction mot à mot," in *Nouveau Roman: hier, aujourd'hui,* ed. by Jean Ricardou and Françoise Van Rossum-Guyon (Paris: UGE, 1972), II, pp. 73-97.

[3]Claude Simon, *Triptyque* (Paris: Minuit, 1973).

[4]Joseph Campbell, *The Hero with a Thousand Faces* (1949; rpt. New York: World, 1956), p. 238.

A SELECTED BIBLIOGRAPHY

The Major Works of Claude Simon:

Le Tricheur. Paris: Sagittaire, 1945.

La Corde raide. Paris: Sagittaire, 1947.

Gulliver. Paris: Calmann-Lévy, 1952.

Le Sacre du printemps. Paris: Calmann-Lévy, 1954.

Le Vent: Tentative de restitution d'un retable baroque. Paris: Minuit, 1957.

L'Herbe. Paris: Minuit, 1958.

La Route des Flandres. Paris: Minuit, 1960.

Le Palace. Paris: Minuit, 1962.

Femmes, sur vingt-trois peintures de Joan Miró. Paris: Maeght, 1966 (limited edition). Reprinted in *Entretiens: Claude Simon,* pp. 169-178.

Histoire. Paris: Minuit, 1967.

La Bataille de Pharsale. Paris: Minuit, 1969.

Orion aveugle. Geneva: Skira, collection "Les sentiers de la création," 1970.

Les Corps conducteurs. Paris: Minuit, 1971.

Triptyque. Paris: Minuit, 1973.

Leçon de choses. Paris: Minuit, 1975.

Books and Articles Consulted:

Albérès, R. M. *Le Roman d'aujourd'hui,* 1960-70. Paris: Albin Michel, 1970.

Albouy, Pierre. *Mythes et mythologies dans la littérature française.* Paris: Armand Colin, 1969.

Apuleius, Lucius. *The Golden Ass.* Ed. Harry C. Schnur. New York: Crowell-Collier, 1962.

Astier, Pierre A. G. *La Crise du roman français et le nouveau réalisme.* Paris: Nouvelles Editions Debresse, 1968.

Auden, W. H. "The Quest Hero." *Perspectives in Contemporary Criticism,* Ed. Sheldon Norman Grebstein. New York: Harper and Row, 1968.

Bachelard, Gaston. *L'Air et les songes.* Paris: Corti, 1943.

—. *La Poétique de la rêverie.* Paris: Presses Universitaires de France, 1968.

—. *La Poétique de l'espace.* Paris: Presses Universitaires de France, 1972.

—. *La Terre et les rêveries de la volonté.* Paris: Corti, 1948.

Barthes, Roland. *Mythologies.* Paris: Seuil, 1957.

Bataille, Georges. *Death and Sensuality: A Study of Eroticism and the Taboo.* New York: Walker, 1962.

—. *L'Erotisme.* Paris: Minuit, 1957.

Beckett, Samuel. *L'Innommable.* Paris: Minuit, 1953.

Berger, Yves. "L'Enfers, Le Temps." *La Nouvelle Revue Française,* 9e année, 97 (January 1961), pp. 95-109.

Bjurstrom, C. G. "Dimensions du temps chez Claude Simon." *Entretiens: Claude Simon.* Ed. Marcel Séguier. Toulouse: Subervie, 1972.

Bloch-Michel, Jean. *Le Présent de l'indicatif.* Paris: Gallimard, 1963.

Bodkin, Maud. *Archetypal Patterns in Poetry.* London: Oxford University Press, 1934.

Brown, Norman O. *Life Against Death: The Psychoanalytical Meaning of History.* Middletown, Connecticut: Wesleyan University Press, 1959.

Campbell, Joseph. *The Hero with a Thousand Faces.* 1949; rpt. New York: World, 1956.

—. *The Masks of God: Creative Mythology.* New York: Viking, 1971.

—. "Mythological Themes in Creative Literature and Art." *Myths, Dreams, and Religion.* Ed. Joseph Campbell. New York: E. P. Dutton, 1970.

—. *Myths to Live By.* New York: Viking, 1972.

—. *The Portable Jung.* New York: Viking, 1971.

Camus, Albert. *Le Mythe de Sisyphe.* Paris: Gallimard, 1942.

—. *Noces suivi de L'Eté.* Paris: Gallimard, 1959.

Champigny, Robert. "Proust, Bergson and other Philosophers." *Proust: A Collection of Critical Essays.* Ed. René Girard. Englewood Cliffs, New Jersey: Prentice-Hall, 1962.

Cirlot, Juan Eduardo. *A Dictionary of Symbols.* Trans. by Jack Sage. New York: Philosophical Library, 1962.

Claude Simon: Analyse, Théorie. Ed. Jean Ricardou. Paris: Union Générale d'Editions, 1975.

Cohen, Gustave. *Essai d'explication du Cimetière marin.* Paris: Gallimard and De Visscher, 1946.

Deleuze, Gilles. *Proust et les signes.* Paris: Presses Universitaires de France, 1971.

Doubrovsky, Serge. "Notes sur la genèse d'une écriture." *Entretiens: Claude Simon.* Ed. Marcel Séguier. Toulouse: Subervie, 1972.

Durand, Gilbert. *Le Décor mythique de La Chartreuse de Parme: Les Structures figuratives du roman stendhalien.* Paris: Corti, 1961.

—. *Les Structures anthropologiques de l'imaginaire: Introduction à l'archetypologie générale.* Paris: Bordas, 1969.

DuVerlie, Claud. *"Amor Interruptus:* The Question of Eroticism or, Eroticism in Question in the Works of Claude Simon." *Sub-Stance,* 8 (Winter, 1974), pp. 21-33.

—. "Interview with Claude Simon." *Sub-Stance,* 8 (Winter, 1974), pp. 3-20.

Edinger, Edward F. *Ego and Archetype: Individuation and the Religious Function of the Psyche.* Baltimore: Penguin, 1973.

Eisenstein, Sergei. *Film Form and The Film Sense.* Trans. by Jay Leyda. New York: Meridian, 1957.

Eliade, Mircea. *Cosmos and History: The Myth of the Eternal Return.* Trans. by Willard R. Trask, 1949; rpt. New York: Harper and Row, 1959.

—. *Images and Symbols: Studies in Religious Symbolism.* Trans. by Willard R. Trask, 1952; rpt. New York: Sheed and Ward, 1969.

—. *Myth and Reality.* Trans. by Willard R. Trask. New York: Harper and Row, 1963.

—. *Myths, Dreams, and Mysteries: The Encounter Between Contemporary Faiths and Archaic Realities.* Trans. by Philip Mairet, 1957; rpt. New York: Harper and Row, 1960.

—. *Rites and Symbols of Initiation: The Mysteries of Birth and Rebirth.* Trans. by Willard R. Trask, 1958; rpt. New York: Harper and Row, 1965.

Feder, Lillian. *Ancient Myth in Modern Poetry.* Princeton: Princeton University Press, 1971.

Fitch, Brian T. "Participe présent et procédés narratifs chez Claude Simon." *Un Nouveau Roman.* Ed. J. H. Matthews. Paris: M. J. Minard, 1964.

Fletcher, John. *Claude Simon and Fiction Now.* London: Calder and Boyars, 1975.

—. "Erotisme et création, ou la mort en sursis." *Entretiens: Claude Simon.* Ed. Marcel Séguier. Toulouse: Subervie, 1972.

—. *New Directions in Literature: Critical Approaches to a Contemporary Phenomenon.* London: Calder and Boyars, 1968.

Foss, Martin. *Symbol and Metaphor in Human Experience.* Princeton: Princeton Unviersity Press, 1949.

Frye, Northrop. *Anatomy of Criticism: Four Essays.* Princeton: Princeton University Press, 1971.

—. *Fables of Identity: Studies in Poetic Mythology.* New York: Harcourt, Brace and World, 1963.

Galand, René. *Baudelaire, poétiques et poésie.* Paris: Nizet, 1969.

Gusdorf, Georges. *Mythe et métaphysique: Introduction à la philosophie.* Paris: Flammarion, 1953.

Harrington, Alan. *The Immortalist: An Approach to the Engineering of Man's Divinity.* New York: Avon, 1970.

Heath, Stephen. *The Nouveau Roman: A Study in the Practice of Writing.* Philadelphia: Temple University Press, 1972.

Henderson, Joseph L. "Ancient Myths and Modern Man." *Man and His Symbols.* Ed. Carl Jung. 1964; rept. New York: Dell, 1968.

Hopper, Stanley Romaine. "Myth, Dream, and Imagination." *Myths, Dreams, and Religion.* Ed. Joseph Campbell. New York: Dutton, 1970.

Huguenin, Jean-René. *Une Autre Jeunesse.* Paris: Seuil, 1965.

Hyman, Stanley Edgar. "The Ritual View of Myth and the Mythic." *Myth: A Symposium.* Ed. Thomas A. Sebeok. Bloomington: Indiana University Press, 1971.

Jacobi, Jolande. *Complex/Archetype/Symbol in the Psychology of C. G.*

Jung. Trans. by Ralph Manheim. New York: Princeton University Press, 1959.

Janvier, Ludovic. "Réponses de Claude Simon à quelques questions écrites de Ludovic Janvier." *Entretiens: Claude Simon.* Ed. Marcel Séguier. Toulouse: Subervie, 1972.

—. *Une Parole exigeante: Le Nouveau Roman.* Paris: Minuit, 1964.

Jean, Raymond. "Les Signes de l'Eros." *Entretiens: Claude Simon.* Ed. Marcel Séguier. Toulouse: Subervie, 1972.

Jiménez-Fajardo, Salvador. *Claude Simon.* Boston: G. K. Hall & Co., 1975.

Jung, C. G. *Collected Works of C. G. Jung: The Archetypes and the Collective Unconscious.* Vol. 9. Trans. by R. F. C. Hull. Princeton: Princeton University Press, 1959.

Langer, Susanne K. *Philosophy in a New Key.* Cambridge: Harvard University Press, 1942.

Leach, Edmund. *Claude Lévi-Strauss.* New York: Viking, 1970.

Leiris, Michel. "Le Réalisme mythologique de Michel Butor." Michel Butor, *La Modification.* Paris: Union Générale d'Editions.

Lévi-Strauss, Claude. *The Raw and the Cooked: Introduction to a Science of Mythology.* Trans. by John and Doreen Weightman. New York: Harper and Row, 1969.

Levitt, Morton P. "Disillusionment and Epiphany: The Novels of Claude Simon." *Critique: Studies in Modern Fiction,* XII, 1 (1970), pp. 43-71.

Loubère, J. A. E. *The Novels of Claude Simon.* Ithaca, New York: Cornell University Press, 1975.

Love, Jean O. *Worlds in Consciousness.* Berkeley: University of California Press, 1970.

Luccioni, Gennie. "Claude Simon: *Histoire.*" *Esprit,* 35e année, 363 (September 1967), pp. 324-328.

Makward, Christiane. "Claude Simon: Earth, Death and Eros." *Sub-Stance*, 8 (Winter, 1974), pp. 35-43.

Mauriac, Claude. *L'alittérature contemporaine.* Paris: Albin Michel, 1969.

Mauron, Charles. *Des Métaphores obsédantes au mythe personnel: Intro-duction à la Psychocritique.* Paris: Corti, 1962.

Mercier, Vivian. *A Reader's Guide to the New Novel.* New York: Farrar, Straus, and Giroux, 1971.

Merleau-Ponty, Maurice. "What is Phenomenology." *European Literary Theory and Practice: From Existential Phenomenology to Structural-ism.* Trans. by Colin Smith. Ed. Vernon W. Gras. New York: Dell, 1973.

Meyerhoff, Hans. *Time in Literature.* Berkeley: University of California Press, 1968.

Minkowski, Eugène. *Lived Time.* Trans. by Nancy Metzel. 1933; rpt. Evanston, Illinois: Northwestern University Press, 1970.

Neumann, Erich. *Amor and Psyche: The Psychic Development of the Feminine.* Trans. by Ralph Manheim. Princeton: Princeton Uni-versity Press, 1956.

—. *Art and the Creative Unconscious: Four Essays.* Trans. by Ralph Manheim. Princeton: Princeton University Press, 1959.

—. *The Great Mother: An Analysis of the Archetype.* Trans. by Ralph Manheim. 1955; rpt. Princeton: Princeton University Press, 1972.

—. *The Origins and History of Consciousness.* Trans. by R. F. C. Hull. 1949; rpt. Princeton: Princeton University Press, 1971.

Nietzsche, Friedrich. *The Birth of Tragedy and The Case of Wagner.* Trans. by Francis Golffing. New York: Doubleday, 1956.

Nouveau Roman: hier. aujourd'hui. 2 vols. Eds. Jean Ricardou and Fran-çoise Van Rossum-Guyon. Paris: Union Générale d'Editions, 1972.

Ovid. *The Metamorphoses.* Ed. Horace Gregory. New York: Viking, 1958.

Pingaud, Bernard. "Sur La Route des Flandres." *Les Temps Modernes,* 16ᵉ année, 178 (fév. 1961), pp. 1026-1037.

Positions et oppositions sur le roman contemporain, proceedings of the Colloque de Strasbourg, "Actes et colloques no. 8." Ed. Michel Mansuy. Strasbourg: Klincksieck, 1971.

Poulet, Georges. *Studies in Human Times.* Trans. by Elliott Coleman. Baltimore: Johns Hopkins Press, 1956.

Progoff, Ira. "Waking Dream and Living Myth." *Myths, Dreams, and Religion.* Ed. Joseph Campbell. New York: Dutton, 1970.

Proust, Marcel. *A la recherche du temps perdu.* 3 vols. Paris: La Pléiade, 1954.

Ricardou, Jean. *Le Nouveau Roman.* Paris: Seuil, 1973.

—. "Un ordre dans la débâcle." *Critique,* 163 (Dec. 1960), pp. 1011-1024.

—. *Pour une théorie du nouveau roman.* Paris: Seuil, 1971.

—. *Problèmes du nouveau roman.* Paris: Seuil, 1967.

Robbe-Grillet, Alain. *Pour un nouveau roman.* Paris: Minuit, 1963.

Ropars-Wuilleumier, Marie-Claire. *De la littérature au cinéma.* Paris: Armand Colin, 1970.

Roudiez, Leon S. *French Fiction Today: A New Direction.* New Brunswick, New Jersey: Rutgers University Press, 1972.

Simon, Claude. "Littérature: Tradition et révolution," *La Quinzaine littéraire* (May 1-15, 1967), pp. 12-13.

Sturrock, John. *The French New Novel: Claude Simon, Michel Butor, Alain Robbe-Grillet.* London: Oxford University Press, 1969.

Valéry, Paul. *Le Cimetière marin.* Ed. Graham Dunstan Martin. Austin: University of Texas Press, 1972.

—. "De Claude Simon à Proust: un exemple d'intertextualité," *Les*

Lettres Nouvelles (September 1972), pp. 107-133.

Van Rossum-Guyon, Françoise. *Critique du roman: Essai sur "La Modification" de Michel Butor.* Paris: Gallimard, 1970.

Vierne, Simone. *Rite, roman, initiation.* Grenoble: Presses Universitaires de Grenoble, 1973.

Weinberg, Bernard. *The Limits of Symbolism.* Chicago: University of Chicago Press, 1966.

Weston, Jessie L. *From Ritual to Romance.* New York: Doubleday, 1957.

Wheelright, Philip. *The Burning Fountain.* Bloomington: Indiana University Press, 1968.

White, John B. *Mythology in the Modern Novel.* Princeton: Princeton University Press, 1971.

Zantz, Emily. *The Aesthetics of the New Novel in France.* Boulder, Colorado: University of Colorado Press, 1968.

INDEX